WINNING SMART BIG
AFTER LOSING

>REVITALIZING PEOPLE, REVIVING ENTERPRISES<

ROB STEARNS

ENCOUNTER BOOKS
SAN FRANCISCO, CALIFORNIA

Published by Encounter Books, an activity of Encounter for Culture and
Education, Inc., a nonprofit tax exempt corporation.

Encounter Books website address: www.encounterbooks.com

Manufactured in the United States and printed on acid-free paper.

The paper used in this publication meets the minimum requirements of
ANSI/NISO
Z39.48-1992 (R 1997) (Permanence of Paper).

FIRST EDITION

Library of Congress Cataloging-in-Publication Data

Stearns, Rob, 1952-
Winning smart after losing big: revitalizing people, reviving enterprises / Rob Stearns.
p. cm.
Includes bibliographical references.
ISBN 1-893554-76-7 (alk. paper)
1. Loss (Psychology). 2. Success--Psychological aspects. I. Title.

BF575.D35 S74 2003
155.9'3 — dc21

2003049133

10 9 8 7 6 5 4 3 2 1

For Katie, Aaron, David, Betty, Sol, and Laurie.
Believers All.

"In adversity, there is strength."
-Julian A. Stearns

CONTENTS

INTRODUCTION   1

CHAPTER ONE: LOSS LEADERS   8

CHAPTER TWO: *YOU* LOSE   15

CHAPTER THREE: YOUR GUIDING PRINCIPLE   24

CHAPTER FOUR: RECOGNIZE YOUR LOSS   30

CHAPTER FIVE: YOUR MIND MENDS YOUR HEART   50

CHAPTER SIX: LET THE OUTSIDE IN   65

CHAPTER SEVEN: WHO, NOT WHAT, YOU ARE   80

CHAPTER EIGHT: HOW TO THINK, WHAT TO DO   86

CHAPTER NINE: *YOU* WIN   98

APPENDIXES: WHAT IF?   100

APPENDIX A: WHAT IF YOU LOSE A LOVED ONE?   102

APPENDIX B: WHAT IF YOU LOSE YOUR HEALTH?   105

APPENDIX C: WHAT IF YOU LOSE A RELATIONSHIP?   108

APPENDIX D: WHAT IF YOU LOSE YOUR JOB?   112

APPENDIX E: WHAT IF YOU LOSE YOUR MONEY?   116

APPENDIX F: THE PRINCIPLES OF WINNING SMART   120

ACKNOWLEDGEMENTS   124

INTRODUCTION

This is a book about losing and winning. You should read this book if you have suffered a loss that hurts you in the stomach or puts a lump in your throat or dries your mouth or weakens your knees. This book is for the bride who is jilted at the altar, the good providing father who loses his job, the gentle mother who aches from a degenerative disease, the athlete who succumbs in front of thousands of fans, the teacher who touches but cannot save the teens in her class, the fireman who carries a lifeless child. This book is for anyone who feels nauseous or aghast or fearful or guilty for suffering the most common of human occurrences, a loss.

I decided to write this book during a bar fight. I admit I wasn't at my best. In fact, I was down for the count. Intoxicated by a two-year entrepreneurial binge, I had relentlessly blown through millions of dollars of savings and borrowings until I had absolutely nothing left. That cash hemorrhage signaled a good time to exit my posh Manhattan aerie for more modest digs in an industrial suburb along the New Jersey Turnpike. Ensconced now at the bottom of a three-floor walk-up, directly across the street from a funeral parlor and several doors down from a tavern, I duked it out with my regular opponent, insomnia. Woozy, I pressed my forehead against the frosty bedroom window, observed the discreet, late night casket delivery to the undertakers, and listened to a concert of splintering wood and shattering glass from the nearby bar.

I scanned the sky for the first smog-pink tinge of dawn, still three time zones east, and mulled again the unanticipated trajectories of my personal and professional past. Imagine swinging on a vine from treetop to treetop and you get the general idea. Now lengthen the vine just enough so that each graceful swoop produces a crash landing on the jungle floor, a good deal of dragging and scraping, then a leg churning lift-off to the next tree. That's really closer to the truth.

I relived giddy highs spliced with numbing lows. I was blessed with loving parents. I watched my father fall ill and die a painful death when I was a boy. I have an Ivy League education and earned graduate degrees in business and law. I lorded in the executive suites of major corporations, fell from grace, and re-ascended. I started small businesses domestically and abroad, but stubbornly persisted in some beyond the point of reason. I earned a fortune, yet made elemental mistakes that financially wiped me out. I married a year out of college, divorced a decade later, and joyfully married again. I attentively and faithfully maintained my body and my health, yet awoke from anesthesia after surgery with a permanently numb and painful face.

I would rather report that the euphoria of winning consistently wafts through all of our lives, that winning glues us together as people. But, you deserve the truth. In real life as you and I know it, losing is the common bond.

We all lose, no matter who we are. Losing is the inescapable phenomenon that intimately connects us. When I walk into a room full of strangers, I have no sure way of knowing if we share common triumphs. But, I know with absolute certainty that we share similar losses. Losing unites us.

Five major losses threaten your happiness, self-esteem, and productivity during your lifetime. Permutations of these plus an infinite number of lesser, but possibly severe, defeats may also bedevil you. But, these are the showstoppers:

1. **Loss of a loved one, such as your spouse, child, or parent**
2. **Loss of your health**
3. **Loss of a relationship, through divorce or separation**
4. **Loss of your job**
5. **Loss of your money**

You can count on suffering at least one of these big losses before you ultimately die. You will probably experience several of them. Each of these losses clobbered me, some more than once. Never easily, I managed to recover from them all.

I tell you this neither to boast nor to suggest that you voluntarily undergo a similar baptism. I'm just letting you know that I lived the messages in this book. I picked myself up, dizzy and dusty, more times than I expected. I never discovered an iota of good in losing. I was never absolutely certain that I could or would rebound. I found each of my recoveries physically demanding, emotionally taxing, and mentally stressful.

After each calamity, I wondered, "Why did that happen?" After each resurgence, I queried, "How did I do that?" And finally, after a series of big losses and big wins, I asked, "Can I avoid loss more effectively? What should I do when I am losing? How should I think and behave, after suffering a loss, to improve my odds of winning again?"

To find out, I thought critically about my own losses and recoveries and then spoke with hundreds of people about how they perceived their defeats and victories. This diverse group of Americans represented many ethnicities, religions, colors, ages, geographies, and occupations. I spoke with literate and unread, wealthy and poor, famous and obscure. Once reassured that I meant no harm, most people conversed eagerly with me about their worst losses and their efforts to recover.

When it comes to losing and winning, you and I already know each other. The specifics of our lives may not completely overlap. But, I bet we have experienced many of the same ups and downs. We work hard. In our endeavors and in our relationships, we invest something more than just our minds and our bodies. Strangers have helped us. Supposed intimates have hurt us. We have ranted at the gods and cursed our luck. Have you ever wondered: "If I'm so smart, how could I screw up so badly?" I have. How about: "I haven't done anything wrong. I don't deserve to lose." Me too. You and I have sunk to the same emotional depths. We have felt the same excruciating hurt, bewilderment, emptiness, and fear.

An empathetic listener recently complimented me by remarking, "You were trained at the school of hard knocks." That comment explains in a nutshell why the topic of losing fascinates me and perhaps you, too. Losing seems poisonous and begets fear of the unknown. Winning after losing seems magical and inspires awe. Yet losing and recovering are incredibly commonplace. We do both everyday. No, I can't claim a degree from the school of hard knocks. Like you, I learned, and continue to learn, at the school of ordinary knocks.

I believe that the universe is not fair or just. I also

believe that the universe is not unfair or unjust. I believe that the universe just exists and we exist in it. I intend no sacrilege by this statement. And, I certainly respect your view of the universe if it differs from mine. But, you and I need a common starting point to talk about losing and winning. Here it is: Losing and winning have nothing to do with fairness and justice. It is possible to try your best, live an honorable life, love your family, worship your God, and still die at the hands of thugs or fanatics.

If you believe that you will be rewarded with a stream of uninterrupted victories as a result of trying hard or being "good," however you define "good," then you are likely to be terribly disappointed. In fact, you must be disappointed already. It started early, didn't it? Remember when you offered to share your dessert and your best friend ate it all? Being good or nice or even try-ing hard will not automatically prevent a loss or guaran-tee a win.

Equally frustrating, losing and winning are not sterile events. We *feel* the loss. We *feel* the win. Sometimes a loss is so suffocating, so disorienting, that another win seems unimaginable. Are you at that point now? Well, the sad fact is that you may be right. You may never win again. There are no guarantees. Forget fairness and justice. You may forever lose and lose and lose. In fact, you may become the first person in the history of the planet to lose all of the time.

Inspirational history abounds with defeat-laden politi-cians, athletes, generals, and scientists who revived, and ultimately triumphed. You already know about the comebacks of Winston Churchill, the buzzer beaters of Michael Jordan, the tenacity of Ulysses S. Grant, and the tireless persistence of Thomas Edison. But, what is the true lesson? That intellect always produces a victory? Not if you were Jimmy Carter. That determination guarantees a win? Not if you were Joe Frazier. That incisiveness ensures a triumph? Not if you were Robert E. Lee. That brilliance dictates immediate glory? Not if you were Galileo.

Popular history favors the winners, often because the winners write the popular history. The truth is, many of history's big losers shared the admirable traits so lauded in the victors. Be inspired by the winners, but remember always, there are no guarantees.

Here, also, I alert you to my style of communicating. This is not a touchy-feely book. You will sense genuine emotion here. But, my intent is not to pull on your heartstrings or lob you an easy fix. This is not five simple solutions to five gigantic catastrophes. I do not expect you to graze on a condescending, dumbed-down compote. Instead, I start with the assumption that you have a lively brain.

Expect no candy-coated words. A "problem" is not a "challenge." It's a problem. A "loss" is not an "opportunity." It's a loss. I'm going to talk to you honestly about losing and what it takes for you to win again. But, I need you to be honest in return. Self-delusionists beware: This book is not for you.

I never use the word "failure" to describe a person who suffers a loss, even a big loss. I regard each loss as an event, not as an overall assessment of a life. Lose your job and you still tuck your kids in at night? How can you call yourself a "failure?" Suffering a loss or a string of losses does not mean that you will never experience another win. Losing once or many times does not mean you are a "failure" as a human being. It means you are normal.

My approach to winning after losing is grounded by an important perspective: I know full well that I am lucky, certainly more fortunate than many, many people. I am not writing this from my deathbed. My wife and sons love me. I enjoy the rights to speak freely, vote freely, and worship freely. I have enough to eat. Yet, I have taken severe beatings in my personal and professional life – severe enough to understand how losing big can decimate your emotions and paralyze your mind.

That's why I ask you to consider this book a conversation between friends, talking earnestly, looking each other straight in the eye. I don't pretend to be your parent, partner, physician, professor, or priest. I don't sit in judgment about your loss. I intend solely to stimulate you to act intelligently, responsibly, and with a sense of purpose when you inevitably lose and afterwards.

This book is alive and interactive on the Internet. When you are intrigued or stimulated by what you read here, you can share your perspectives and experiences with other readers and with me. I invite you to log on and contribute to the Forum discussions highlighted at the end of each Chapter.

Five major losses and trillions of minor ones are out there waiting for you. I'm eager to applaud your victories.

Did this Chapter stimulate you? Share your specific thoughts, questions, and experiences with other readers of **WINNING SMART** AFTER LOSING BIG by logging onto www.robstearns.com. Then, go to the Forum page, select "Introduction" from the Forum List, and join the discussion.

CHAPTER ONE
LOSS LEADERS

I can think of two practical reasons to explain why you are reading this book. Purely as an individual, you want to improve your odds of winning after suffering a major personal loss. Or, as a leader, you want to improve your corporation's or institution's chances to recover after suffering a major enterprise loss. Either way, as an individual or as a leader of individuals, you seek insight regarding the phenomena of defeat and subsequent triumph.

Enterprise loss and personal loss are closely related. In fact, they are the same. You may find this hard to accept, particularly if you believe that personal loss is always "worse" or "more important" than enterprise loss. But, compare the loss of a war by a freedom-loving country versus the death of any one of its soldiers during the war. Which is worse, the enterprise loss or the personal loss – the loss of civil liberties in the defeated country or the death of one its defenders?

Certainly, this question can arouse passionate debate. Your view may depend on whether you are a citizen now enslaved in the defeated nation, one of the victors, or the dead soldier's parent. And that's my point. All discussions about loss distill to how a specific loss affects a specific individual. Distinctions between enterprise loss and personal loss get muddled and eventually disappear.

Only people lose and win.

This fundamental theme runs through my entire discussion with you. I speak to you, as an individual, because losing and winning are uniquely personal. And, I speak to you, as a leader, because that's precisely who you are. At the very least, and really at the very most, you are President of your own life.

Enterprises – business organizations, charities, athletic teams, even nations – do not experience victory and defeat. Enterprises are essentially empty vessels, lifeless and inert. The headlines may state that GoGo Industries lost sales. But the truth is, the salespeople at GoGo sold fewer products, maybe due to inferior design by GoGo's engineers or careless assembly by GoGo's factory workers. The Yankees never won a World Series. The ballplayers who pitched and hit and fielded did. The United States did not win World War II. The women and men who worked in the factories and bled in the foxholes did. When I say enterprise loss or enterprise win, I always mean the loss or win experienced collectively by the individuals who populate the enterprise.

This is more than semantics. It explains why recovery from enterprise loss and recovery from personal loss are identical processes. Enterprises are more productive when their people recognize that losing and winning are human, not institutional, phenomena. People who understand losing are better equipped to recover when they lose individually. People who understand losing and who lose while participating in an enterprise are better prepared to reorient their enterprise. Revitalized people revive enterprises, not the other way around.

As a result, personal loss and enterprise leadership are inextricably intertwined. You lead an enterprise more effectively when you understand the phenomenon of losing. Here's why: You are primed to recover personally from loss. You are equipped to help other people in the enterprise to recover from their losses. And, most importantly, your clearheaded familiarity with defeat prepares you to inspire people to act, voluntarily, to create a recovery for their enterprise.

"Voluntarily" is the key word. A dictator is not a true leader of his countrymen if torture is his enforcer. An autocratic corporate officer is not a true leader of her employees if threatened firings are her prod. A bullying parent is not a true leader of his family if a backhand slap makes his point. True leadership occurs only when the followers have the option not to follow.

So, why do followers voluntarily follow true leaders?

Think personally. If you are a leader in an enterprise – President of the United States, Chairperson of your local PTA – why do you suppose you were elected or appointed to your leadership position? Assume, for example, that you are the Chief Executive Officer of a large company. How did you get the job? Were you really so much smarter or imaginative or productive than the other executives vying for the top spot? Possibly. But, I doubt it. Most likely, all of the contenders for the job were smart and imaginative and productive. Your selection was probably a pretty close call. I bet the dispositive factor was: Your Board of Directors and the previous Chief Executive trusted you more than your rivals.

Trust anoints leaders. Your designation as a leader in any enterprise affirms the trust of the people who selected you. Similarly, the element of trust explains why soldiers follow sergeants into battle, why parishioners follow priests in prayer, why superstar athletes follow their coach's plays, why you as a child believed, rather than just obeyed, your parents. Voluntary followers follow because they trust their leaders. And equally as important, though more difficult to say, voluntary followers follow because they trust their fellow followers. Effective leaders create, require, and use trust. Trust that flows upward from followers to leaders empowers the leaders to lead. Trust that flows downward from leaders to followers enables the leaders to delegate. Trust that flows laterally among followers endows the leaders with team play and cohesion of purpose within the enterprise. Trust is the absolute circulating blood of leadership.

But, aspiring and existing leaders share a big problem: Genuine trust is tough to earn and hard to keep. It cannot be manufactured or bought. Yes, uniforms, lapel pins, and flags do provide a sense of familiarity and unity. But, these physical cloaks only symbolize trust. They are temporary, disposable. Real trust cannot be shed at night.

Sometimes, enterprise leaders try to build trust via exercises designed to proxy real world experiences. Here's a true example: Every year, a well-known corporation gathers its two hundred most senior executives at a two-day, leadership development conference. At a recent session, the attendees were marched out onto a large field. There, they found three, thirty-foot high telephone poles securely planted upright in the ground. From the sides of each pole protruded a series of metal foot- and handholds, running from bottom to top.

The executives were fitted into safety harnesses, then instructed to climb to a pole's summit and leap off. Other executives, while awaiting their turns to climb, manned the ropes that ran through pulleys atop the poles and ultimately to the jumpers' safety rigs. The point of the exercise? Each jumper was forced to "trust" the ground crew to pull on their ropes hard enough to stop the pre-splatter plummet.

Totally nuts. And, counter-productive to boot. Contrived risk-taking produces about as much genuine trust as a secret handshake. The rah-rah excitement of the moment quickly erodes to sheepishness, then resentment at the superficiality of the experience. Enduring trust cannot be created on demand.

Instead, genuine trust evolves when leaders and followers, together, survive and conquer the impediments to moving an enterprise forward. Commingled tears more than common laughter fortify these journeys. And often, the most significant odysseys begin with shared defeats.

The forging of trust
occurs in the crucible of loss.

For you, as a leader, moments of loss are astonishingly important. These are precisely the instants when you earn or dispel the trust of the people in your enterprise. These are unquestionably the seminal trials of your judgment, wisdom, fortitude, vision, patience, and compassion that determine with clarity whether you merit the trust of your followers and the trust of yourself. Leaders derive trust by understanding and overcoming loss.

Understanding loss is easier than overcoming loss. Understanding loss simply means that you, alone, mentally comprehend the phenomenon of defeat. Probably, just by dint of experiencing life's daily vicissitudes, you already understand a good deal about losing. Perhaps you have even reflected on the topic personally and in the context of your enterprise. If so, you are likely to find some of my messages familiar. "I know that," you may say after reading a passage that strikes you right. And, that's fine. But, understanding the phenomenon of losing is only the first step in the process of winning smart.

Overcoming loss requires more than understanding, more than mental gymnastics. Overcoming personal loss requires that you adjust your behavior. Overcoming enterprise loss requires that you, as a leader, adjust the behavior of the individuals in your enterprise by stimulating them to act in concert to produce a victory.

Winning smart is a process that celebrates behavior change in individuals when and after they lose. For enterprise leaders, this process encourages you to:

1. **Understand the phenomenon of losing so that you can adjust your own behavior.** Unfortunately, that's not enough to create wins for your enterprise.

2. **Codify your knowledge and standards of conduct.** Your followers need to know what you know. At minimum, they need to comprehend the standards of behavior that you expect them to adopt during and after losing.

3. **Communicate what you know.** Distribute your standards to everyone in your enterprise. Encourage the people in your organization to ask questions about your code so that you clarify and they better understand your rationale and intent.

4. **Prescribe specific, remedial action steps.** Behave true to your standards of conduct so that the people in your enterprise see and emulate your behavior. Welcome the creation of trust.

5. **Reward the individuals in your enterprise who adopt your standards, adjust their behaviors, and strive to implement your action steps.** To motivate individuals to adopt your code, tie rewards directly to the behavior changes that you want to occur.

Fundamentally, this book is the codification portion of winning smart. It is an easily distributable, annotated code of behavior. I offer it to you, as an individual, to fortify your thoughts and personal conduct. I offer it to you, as a leader, to help you define and coalesce the behavior of the people in your enterprise, joined in the pursuit of a common goal.

As I talk with you in the following chapters, I focus on personal loss because every enterprise loss is essentially a collection of losses suffered by individuals. If you understand personal loss, you will understand enterprise loss. As an enterprise leader, you try zealously to prevent people from losing. And when you cannot, you earn your pay and affirm your leadership by inspiring and directing their recoveries. You lead for the good of your enterprise. But really, you lead for the good of the individuals in your enterprise.

Did this Chapter stimulate you? Share your specific thoughts, questions, and experiences with other readers of **WINNING SMART** AFTER LOSING BIG by logging onto www.robstearns.com. Then, go to the Forum page, select "Chapter One: Loss Leaders" from the Forum List, and join the discussion.

CHAPTER TWO
YOU LOSE

When I say "win" or "lose," you understand me immediately. But, do you really know what I mean? We use these words so frequently that their definitions seem hardwired into our brains. Exploring this circuitry, however, reveals two surprises. First, everyone's wiring is not the same – our definitions of victory and defeat actually vary. And second, we are not hardwired after all – we can change, or at least try to change, our perceptions of winning and losing as well as our actions during and after a loss.

This flexibility complicates our discussion right off the bat. As we talk, we need to reconfirm occasionally that we understand each other's meaning of "win" and "lose." But, this inconvenience is well worth the trouble. Our flexibility enables us to win smart, as individuals, facing unique circumstances.

Here are my general definitions of winning and losing.

You can win in two ways:

1. **If you get what you want, you win.** For example, if you want a promotion and get it, you win. Or,

2. **If you don't get what you don't want, you win.** For example, if you don't want to catch pneumonia and you don't catch pneumonia, you win.

You can lose in two ways:

1. **If you don't get what you want, you lose.** For example, if you want to make the game winning shot and miss it, you lose. Or,

2. **If you get what you don't want, you lose.** For example, if you want safe sex, but contract HIV during the act, you lose.

What you want and what you don't want are purely personal. Laws and social customs obviously influence what you want and what you don't want. But, for many varied reasons, your choices may not always coincide with the preferences of your family, your neighbors, your employer, or even your government. I make no judgment here about what you should want and what you should not want. I make no assumption about whether you are "right" if you win or "wrong" if you lose.

My point is simply: Most of the time, you choose – sometimes knowingly, sometimes implicitly – specific definitions of winning and losing. You craft precise definitions that are uniquely yours. To you, winning and losing are what you believe they are. And as a result, you anoint yourself with the unique responsibility for bearing the consequences that flow from your personal definitions of victory and defeat.

Consider this true example: Rolland and Kris are both superb artists. Rolland chooses to define winning in terms of how much money he earns by selling his paintings. For Rolland, winning requires income production. In contrast, Kris chooses to define winning in terms of the personal joy he receives by creating beautiful landscapes. For Kris, winning requires no sales at all. Rolland does not want to live the life of a starving artist. Kris does not want to pander to the vogues of artistic taste. Each artist argues, correctly, that his definition is "right." Both of their definitions of winning and losing are purely personal.

How each artist defines winning and losing ultimately determines whether each artist regards himself as a winner or a loser. If Rolland produces beautiful landscapes that no one buys, then he perceives that he has lost and is likely to be distraught. If Kris cannot capture sunsets to his creative satisfaction, yet sells enough paintings to become a popular icon, then he also believes that he has lost and is also likely to be distraught. Your perception of winning and losing determines whether you see a winner or a loser when you look in the mirror.

Many situations require you to consider several definitions of winning and losing. Sometimes, you can accommodate and balance complementary definitions. But often, the choices conflict, cannot be reconciled, or at the very least, require you to assign priorities.

In the case of the artists, Rolland wants to earn money with his talent. If he discovers that art buyers gobble up paintings of red and purple tulips, he has no qualms about reconciling his definitions of commercial win and artistic win. Faster than oil paint dries, he launches his "Bulb Period" and creates masterpieces containing red and purple tulips.

Alternatively, if Kris becomes infatuated with yellow daffodils growing by the banks of a frothy blue brook, he strives to capture the essential beauty of that scene. Tweaking the sales potential of the canvas by inserting a couple of red and purple tulips makes no sense to him. To Kris, the artistic win transcends the commercial win and he elects not to combine the two.

In your everyday life, you frequently make choices that actually express your definitions of winning and losing. Have you ever opted to spend more time on the job rather than at home with your family, or visa versa? Have you ever chosen to keep your word rather than expediently break a promise? Have you ever violated your diet to enjoy a scrumptious ice cream sundae?

Sure you have.

From a plethora of potential wins and losses, you eventually determine which wins are most valuable to you and which losses are most onerous to you. You select what you want the most and what you want to avoid the most. Your selections – your specific definitions of winning and losing – determine ultimately your perception of whether you have won or lost.

Possibly, you may commit egregious errors of judgment, misinterpret facts, use incorrect data, or bow to the will of other people as you develop your definitions. Your methodology for reconciling and ranking your definitions may be flawed. But, to you, your perception of truth is paramount. Your belief in your definitions of winning and losing is at the absolute heart of whether you regard yourself as a winner or a loser in any given situation.

Assuming that you are *compos mentis*, you choose your definitions of winning and losing voluntarily. You, of your own free will, define what victory and defeat mean to you. Your definitions may cause you great difficulties if they are contrary to societal norms or laws. As a civil rights activist, for example, you may choose to disobey the law and go to jail as a consequence. *You* decide that adhering to your principles is a win, a win more valuable than staying out of prison. Similarly, if you are gay and announce your sexual preference, you may attract innuendo and insult. *You* decide that coming out is a win, a win more valuable than universal acceptance.

Again, I offer no legal or social counsel here. My point is solely that *you* choose how to define victory and defeat. *You* choose which wins and losses are most significant to *you*. You may be swayed by others. But, in the end, *you* decide.

Every win/lose situation that you experience during your lifetime really consists of a continuum, illustrated below in Exhibit 1.

Exhibit 1: Win/Lose Continuum

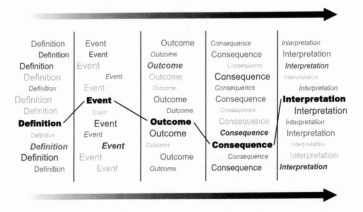

Each continuum is unique and situation specific. You define winning and losing at the front end of each flow. Sometimes, your definitions relate to hypothetical events – some events occur, others do not. Regardless, these events and non-events produce outcomes. From out-comes flow consequences. You interpret outcomes and their consequences by using your definitions to determine if you should declare victory or defeat.

This continuum – definition, event, outcome, conse-quence, interpretation – is important. Starkly put, win-ning or losing depends entirely on how you shape the five elements of this flow. Here are the *only* ways to influence whether you win or lose:

1. Change your definitions of winning and losing for any particular event.
2. Alter the course of an event.
3. Change the outcome of an event after the event concludes.
4. Adjust the consequences of an event's outcome.
5. Interpret the event's outcomes and consequences accurately and honestly – or not.

Consider this example: You earn your living by entering data into a computer. One morning, as you type on the keyboard, agonizing pain shoots through your right wrist. The pain persists for days. You cannot work. Worried, you schedule an appointment with your doctor.

As you approach your doctor's office, you are really at the beginning of a win/lose continuum. Ostensibly, you will incur a win or a loss as a result of your visit. So, how do you define losing? Does losing mean "a lifetime of chronic pain" if you continue to type? Or, "loss of your job" because you cannot type? Or, something else? How you define losing establishes how you may act later in the continuum and, ultimately, whether you believe that you have suffered a loss.

The doctor squeezes your wrist and asks, "Does that hurt?" How you answer, may alter the course of the examination – the event. If you say "Yes," the doctor may diagnose you with Carpel Tunnel Syndrome and advise you to stop typing on the keyboard. Bye-bye job. But, the doctor may also prescribe treatment. Bye-bye pain. Answering "No" to the doctor's question establishes a different course of events. Either response affects whether you win or lose according to your earlier definitions.

Assume you do answer "yes" and the doctor suggests that you stop working at the keyboard. You may respond, "But, the pain is not so severe. Can I continue to type if I take a regular dose of aspirin?" After the examination and the diagnosis, you try to change the physician's recommendation – the outcome.

If your doctor responds, "Sure, give it a try," you avoid losing – if you defined losing as "loss of your job." But, suppose your doctor says, "If you don't stop using the keyboard, you will suffer permanent nerve damage." You lose. Time to look for a new job – the consequence of heeding your doctor's advice. But, suppose you keep your job by convincing your employer to permit you to use voice-activated software instead of keyboard input. You don't lose. Yet.

Unfortunately, the voice-activated software is error prone and slow. Your job performance deteriorates. Your employer fires you. You lose your job because you cannot type – your honest interpretation. But, suppose you rationalize and say, "I hated that job. I'm glad I don't have to work there anymore." Did you interpret the flow of the win/loss continuum accurately? No. Did you really lose? According to your original definition, yes.

But, what if you really did hate your job? Suppose getting sacked motivates you to land your dream job. Isn't that really a win? Of course it is – but not because, with the benefit of hindsight, you no longer define "losing your job" as a loss. In truth, it is a win because you started a second win/lose continuum and defined "obtain a new job" as a win.

You can see that winning and losing can get pretty complicated. Even everyday situations contain complex permutations. That's why the win/lose continuum is helpful. It distills winning and losing to an understand-able flow. It helps you think.

Changing your definitions of winning and losing, at the start of the continuum, is completely within your control. You may consider some of your definitions untouchable, cast in stone. No problem. But often, you tailor your def-initions to specific circumstances. The beginning of each continuum provides a fresh chance to establish what win-ning and losing mean to you.

Perhaps, you also enjoy complete control over the course of events, outcomes, and consequences. Probably, you do not. Too often and through no fault of your own, you may passively witness events spiraling out of your control, producing undesirable outcomes followed by distasteful consequences. Generally, you only partially control this portion of the continuum.

Interpretation, the final element of the continuum, seems completely within your control. But, you really control only your choice to interpret honestly or not. You can filter outcomes and consequences through your original definitions to determine if you won or lost. Or, you can "spin" your interpretation to shade the truth. Spinning really means altering your initial definitions, *at the end* of the continuum. This is the equivalent of mov-ing the finish line after the race is over.

Honest interpretation requires that you hold your def-initions constant for any single continuum. How you define winning and losing at the beginning of the contin-uum ultimately dictates whether you should declare vic-tory or defeat at the end. If you are intellectually honest, interpretation is completely *out* of your control.

Your understanding of your unique, win/lose continu-um and your range of control shapes your recovery after a major debacle. You can completely control your defini-tions of losing and winning. But, that's it. Your control over the other elements of the continuum varies.

You win when you exercise enough control over a continuum to create a victory. Your best chances to influence a continuum occur at points that are receptive or vulnerable to your control. My intent is to help you find those points. When you do, my intent is to help you think and behave so that you exercise control effectively. Winning smart is a process of improving your odds – by guiding your thoughts and directing your actions to the points on a win/lose continuum where you can exert the greatest influence.

Did this Chapter stimulate you? Share your specific thoughts, questions, and experiences with other readers of **WINNING SMART** AFTER LOSING BIG by logging onto www.robstearns.com. Then, go to the Forum page, select "Chapter Two: *You* Lose" from the Forum List, and join the discussion.

CHAPTER THREE
YOUR GUIDING PRINCIPLE

I want to provide you with an essential message right now. Everything else I share with you about how to win after suffering a loss builds on this most important maxim. Conceptually, it is common wisdom. Its value derives not from its novelty, but from its truth. I ask you to think about it differently, more acutely, than ever before.

When you are knocked down, you must force yourself to get back up.

Adopt this guiding principle as your own. Say it with your name: "Michael's Law" or "Jennifer's Law." Own it and believe it.

Unless you are extraordinarily lucky, you will never ever win again until you summon whatever strength or courage you have and get back up. If you are totally on empty with no reserves, you must will yourself to get back up. If you are knocked down while you are attempting to rise, you must get back up again. You must get back up, no matter how embarrassing, no matter how tortured.

After every loss, you must force yourself to get back up.

Now what does this really mean? When you lose, you rarely get literally knocked down. So what's the point of the analogy?

It's a vision of losing that is graphic and easy to understand. You and I know that most of the major losses you incur in real life are much more abstract and complex. But, how do you begin to gather your senses when your crops wither from a drought or your husband leaves you for another woman? Where do you start? You begin by simplifying, by understanding where you are: knocked down flat on your back. In your own mind, see yourself spread-eagled. Recognize that for whatever the cause or reason, you are down.

Your life is comprised of millions of personal defeats and victories. Of course, you don't consciously register these events as losses or wins. You'd go crazy tallying up a day's worth of them. Most are inconsequential. Yet, you do experience and react to them. Take a look at Exhibit 2, on the next page, to visualize this series of wins and losses.

During any period in your lifetime, most of your losses and wins impact only your subconscious. These losses are mostly inconveniences and do not require calculated responses. Your react automatically, instinctively. An example: Your toddler daughter develops a messy, runny nose just as you are about to take her to nursery school. You wipe her nose with a tissue and continue out the door. Consider this the benign background noise of losing.

Sometimes, you consciously note a loss or a win. You react with a sense of heightened awareness, perhaps with a brief feeling of disappointment or elation. A loss at this level usually requires a more thoughtful response. An example: Your pre-teen daughter comes home from grade school with a poor report card. Consider this the tolerable, though discordant, noise of losing.

And occasionally, you experience a loss or a win that stops you in your tracks. You reel with reaction, perhaps with shivering grief, perhaps with euphoric pleasure. A loss of this magnitude demands a disciplined, wise response. An example: Your teenage daughter departs from her high school, but never returns home. On the audible scale, consider this thunder.

Exhibit 2: A Lifetime of Wins and Losses

Win

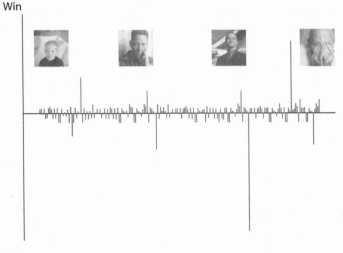

Loss

Sometimes, a big loss is comprised of a series, a seemingly unending series, of small losses. But generally, a big loss comes as a single shock: the diagnosis of cancer, the death of your spouse, the dissolution of your fortune. A big loss rocks your very being. A big loss may obliterate years of hard work, erase a lifetime of self-confidence, or crush your sense of self-worth. A big loss may cause despair, self-disappointment, and self-hate. Who you are, your place in the world, and your reason for living become extraordinarily unclear after a major personal defeat.

Fortunately, every loss, even a big loss, is a single event. True, you may experience the ramifications of a loss for a lifetime. But, the loss itself is over the moment it occurs. Appreciate the temporal nature of a loss. And, separate the act of losing from the consequences of losing.

Distinguishing between the event of losing and the consequences of losing is extremely important. Many people are paralyzed after a big loss because they dread losing again. But, it's not losing that they really fear. It's the consequences of losing. Losing may be painful and humiliating, for sure. But, the real problem with losing is that it obligates you to do something that you absolutely do not want to do. Want to test your endurance after a triple bypass surgery? Want to re-earn your fortune after a spasm of poor investing? Want to go through the dating ritual after your girlfriend says *adios*? Want to face a curious press corps after that dropped pass in the end zone? Want to apologize to your wife for gambling away the rent? Want to discipline your child after he gets busted for dope? Want to examine your loss so honestly that you may determine it was mostly your doing?

The consequences of a loss exist whether you get back up or not. But, for you to deal proactively and positively with these consequences, you must first deal constructively with yourself. As a first step, stop, forever, fearing the literal event of losing. To do that, recognize that each loss is a single event and believe that no loss, no matter how huge, dooms you to an eternity of repeating losses.

Your immediate mission after suffering a loss is to create a win.

Envision yourself attempting to get up on your feet. More than that, see yourself rising, perhaps wobbly, perhaps stumbling, but ultimately rising to a standing position. See yourself getting back up. Why? Because, getting back up is a win. It is your first win after a loss. It is essential. It proves to you that the loss was a single event. It proves to you that you are capable of winning. You must force yourself to get back up.

The odd paradox is that when you get back up, you re-expose yourself to the risk of losing and winning again. Getting back up does not mean undoing the loss. Getting back up means voluntarily re-entering the fray. This self-willed re-exposure to losing and winning is an essential precursor to recovering from a big loss.

You do this automatically in your everyday life when you suffer small losses. Consider what happens when you spot a parking space and just before you enter it, another car zips in. You don't leave the parking lot and go home. You don't wait until the other driver returns to his car after several hours of shopping so that you can occupy that very space. Instead, you begrudgingly accept the loss and drive onward, taking the risk that you will find another place to park. You naturally re-expose yourself to losing and winning after small losses. But, you must deliberately will yourself to do it after big losses. You must force yourself to get back up.

When I say, "You must force yourself to get back up," I do mean *you* and only you. This is not a team effort. No one, no matter how well intentioned, can be your substitute. The cold truth is that recovering from a big loss requires you to recommit to yourself. This is not an act of contrition or false bravado. This is an extremely personal, quiet reaffirmation of yourself in your own eyes. In the quiet and the dark of night, alone with your demons and your inner voice, acknowledge your doubts, your fears, your anger, and then promise yourself that you will get back up.

Did this Chapter stimulate you? Share your specific thoughts, questions, and experiences with other readers of **WINNING SMART** AFTER LOSING BIG by logging onto www.robstearns.com. Then, go to the Forum page, select "Chapter Three: Your Guiding Principle" from the Forum List, and join the discussion.

CHAPTER FOUR
RECOGNIZE
YOUR LOSS

It's very cold in the train, easily below freezing. Icy, winter drafts from the punctured windows numb my toes. As we pass from dusk to dark, one naked red bulb provides quivering illumination for the exit door at the rear of the car. No other lights glow, but the moon phosphoresces my breath.

I'm lying on a thin vinyl pad atop a wooden slab of a berth. Underneath a scratchy, stained, maroon blanket, I'm fully dressed: insulated long underwear, pants, sweater, socks, overcoat, and ski cap. No pillow. My three Russian traveling partners snore. I'm freezing as I listen to the hiss of the wind and wince to the cadence of every rail joint.

I'm heading east, miles and miles from Moscow, to a former Soviet "secret city." This particular enclave existed to isolate research scientists working on Soviet defense projects. Barely a year prior to this train ride, I watched the implosion of the Soviet empire on television. Bored with observing, eager to participate, I left my position as the head of a well-known investment banking group to become a farmer – a farmer of technology. My entrepreneurial intent: Identify and acquire seedlings of Soviet science, fertilize them with Western development capital, and grow them into a bounty of commercial products.

Well fortified with experience, zeal, and connections, I established offices and employees in the former Soviet Union on the frontier of capitalism.

On the day before boarding the train, at a meeting in a lecture hall in a prestigious Russian scientific academy, I listen to my translator's simultaneous recounting of the fourteenth or fifteenth presentation of the day. The dank room smells of diesel, wet wool, Turkish tobacco, and body odor. I have a terrific headache.

At the podium stands a thirtyish doctorate of electrical engineering. For his entire professional life, he helped develop missile guidance systems. Today, he reveals the results of his after hours' labor of love. I listen carefully as he explains his invention. He holds a plastic box about the size of a pack of cigarettes in his left hand and looks at it while he talks. He is animated, proud, but not boastful. He has invented a thermostatic device that will permit kitchen refrigerator freezers to self-defrost automatically. He is oblivious to the existence of self-defrosting freezers in the West.

At the edge of democracy, political instability reigns. Russian tanks circled and bombarded the Parliament building not long before my train ride. Now, in the cold and dark, I bite off a piece of tough greasy sausage and think about the science I might see tomorrow. I am on a treasure hunt. I am losing.

How you think about losing and winning absolutely influences how often you win and how quickly you win after a major loss. Suffering a big loss, then creating a victory, is uniquely personal. Selflessness, so vital in team play, is far less important for producing a personal win. In fact, the opposite is true. To truly understand losing and to rebound from a big loss, you need a healthy dose of self

– particularly self-honesty, self-respect, and self-reliance. Self-honesty is telling yourself the truth, no matter how awful. Self-respect is treating yourself fairly and with compassion. Self-reliance is assigning responsibility to no one but yourself for improving your current situation.

Unsurprisingly, the process of losing erodes these traits precisely when you need them the most. Your mind grasps winning easily. But, losing confuses and disorients you. Often, while losing, your mind denies the loss or makes excuses for the loss or conjures a win from the loss. To overcome this dizziness, you must mentally revitalize these traits to view your situation with dispassionate objectivity. I know this is extremely difficult. I could not do it on the train in Russia.

Summoning the three traits of self-honesty, self-respect, and self-reliance allows you to adjust your traditional thinking about losing and winning. In the United States today, the premise that "winning is everything" dominates politics, business, sports, entertainment, education, and most social relations. Take a stroll past the Little League field on Saturday morning and listen to the hollering coaches. Sit in on an issue oriented Congressional caucus meeting or a major corporation's Board of Directors meeting and witness the need to vanquish the competition. Observe the "put down" humor of the most popular sitcoms. Note how "reality television" copies a formula that enticed Romans to the Coliseum centuries ago.

Clearly, this obsession with winning has many positives. It is the essence of fair and spirited competition. It encourages superior performance in all endeavors. It establishes a rational pattern for reward.

But at the same time, this fixation produces a mental blind spot that will hurt you if you fail to recognize it. If you demand of yourself that you win at all costs, then you run the extreme risk of failing to perceive situations where you absolutely cannot win.

To prevent a loss, you must recognize first that you are losing.

Adjust your mindset to improve your odds of winning. Realize that in some instances, suffering a loss, even a big loss, is preferable to prolonging a futile struggle that inevitably results in the same or bigger loss. Yes, this runs against the dogma of "Don't give up the ship!" However, weigh the stigma of giving up the ship against the likelihood and consequences of going down with the ship.

Winning is not going down with the ship. Winning is wheeling the ship out of danger. And, if sinking is certain, then winning is getting your dependents and yourself safely off the ship. To win, you must survive. To survive and win again, sometimes you must choose when to lose.

The "win or die" credo causes you to persist in situations where the probabilities of winning are so low that you would be far better off to accept defeat, regroup, and try anew. And ultimately, this blind spot warps your judgment so severely that you cannot determine when you have lost. So befuddled, you refuse to admit to yourself that you have lost. You simply can't believe it.

Here's a true example: A friend of mine is a well-respected diamond merchant. His clients travel from around the world to purchase exquisite jewelry in his exclusive offices high in a Manhattan tower. His family was in the diamond trade for several generations before him and he thoroughly understood the business long before earning a graduate degree from a leading business school. For more than two decades, he built his enterprise conservatively, never overstretched financially, and always served his clientele with integrity. He treated his dozen, well-trained employees with respect and they, in turn, treated his clients with special care.

About a year ago, my friend wanted additional capital to grow his business. He intended to acquire more diamonds so that he would have more jewelry on hand to offer to visiting clients. He launched a search to obtain investment in his company. His sales were growing, though not as briskly as in recent years. The few potential investors he found adopted a wait-and-see approach.

While the general economy cooled, my friend interpreted the slowing of his sales as a sign that he needed a more diverse inventory. He borrowed heavily to finance the purchase of more gems and continued to search for investors. But, his sluggish sales growth and increased borrowings made potential investors wary. He began to lay off staff. He delayed payment of his bills. He fell delinquent on his interest charges. After several months, his lenders seized his entire inventory. Unsecured creditors began a series of lawsuits. With funds depleted and no inventory to sell, my friend put his business into bankruptcy and filed for personal bankruptcy as well. A life's work, gone.

Visiting New York for a meeting, I noticed a display case in a chic hotel prominently advertising my friend's business. Not knowing the severity of his troubles, I telephoned him to say hello and tease him about his obvious success. In an oddly strained voice, he invited me to visit. When I stepped off the elevator, no security guard stood at his suite's entrance. Instead, a young woman responded to my buzz, unlocked the door, and ushered me inside. No telephones rang. No employees manned the sales or accounting or assaying rooms. Walking to my friend's office, we passed by rows of glass display cases, once filled with diamonds of sizzling brilliance, now dark and bare.

My friend sat behind his desk, dressed as usual in a dark suit, obviously tired. For half an hour, he lucidly explained the events of the past several months. Then, amid a silent, inert office strewn with the detritus of a financial meltdown, he asked an irrational question of the first order: "Do you think that it will be easier to obtain investor funds, now that the business is bankrupt and has no debt?"

Astounding! How could anybody ask this question? The business was gone. There was nothing left. There was no business. It was over. But, if you understand the "Don't give up the ship!" blind spot, you can understand my friend's query. Besieged and saddled with a blurred vision of losing and winning, he reacted predictably. In his own mind, he still did not believe that he had lost.

The blind spot induces a mindset that stalls your recovery from a loss. It prevents you from winning because you misdirect all of your energies and efforts on the past, flailing to win in a situation that is already, unquestionably lost.

To create a win after a loss, you must recognize first that you have lost.

So how do you know? How do you know when you are losing? And, equally as perplexing: How do you know that an apparent loss cannot be averted and reversed into a win? And most important of all: How do you know when you have truly suffered a loss?

Every day, you observe yourself and your passage through your life's small and large events. In fact, you are more than an observer. You are a critic. You make judgments about these events. You assess your own performance and progress. You keep score. You measure. You measure instinctively and very frequently. These measurements form your internal view of whether you are losing or winning in any particular situation. You measure all day long and most of the time you are right. But, when you are losing big, accurate measurement becomes elusive and more prone to error.

To realize truly that you are losing, to assess fairly the probabilities of averting a loss, and to understand unequivocally that you have suffered a loss, you need objective, clearly defined, measurement criteria. Accurate appraisal of events and yourself requires straightforward, trustworthy reference points to benchmark your performance and progress. These vital measurement criteria should unambiguously blare "Win!" or "Loss!"

As you plan to participate in a major activity, identify the criteria that you will use to judge whether you are winning or losing. In spontaneous activities too, you need an intelligent way to gauge your position. Your criteria should be fact-based and easily ascertained. Identifying a loss is tough enough without complicating the measurement process. You need precise and user-friendly standards.

Write the criteria down. Writing forces you to be specific and equips you with a stress-resistant reference document. Regard your list of measurements as a contract and pledge to honor it. Use these measurement criteria, consciously and frequently, as you progress through any major win/lose continuum. And, here's where self-honesty becomes so essential:

To recognize when you have lost, you must consider your measurement standards so sacred that you do not ignore them or change them conveniently in times of crisis.

It's tempting to adjust your measurement criteria midstream. The rationale for this adjustment seems so compelling: Once engaged in an event, you think you understand your predicament better. Why not change your measurement standards when you are equipped with this greater knowledge?

I disagree with this enticing logic. And you should, too. In theory, it sounds fine. But, in the real world of losing and winning, it is not a universal truth. Here's why: When you are suffering a loss, especially a big loss, passion and emotion often obscure your ability or desire to measure. Most losses produce stress. A major loss can provoke a full-blown mental crisis. Almost no one thinks deliberately while under the pressure of losing big. Mid-loss and post-loss, your views of your world and of yourself are rarely objective and almost always wrong. What a terrible time to forsake trustworthy reference points!

Return with me to the train in central Russia. When I began this entrepreneurial adventure, I established objective measurements to gauge my progress. I formulated a budget with spending ceiling. I established a timeline. I identified key occurrences that would signal wins or losses. Yet as my odyssey progressed, I altered every one of these measurements mid-stream, believing that I had a better perspective than when I started. Emotion undeniably influenced my thinking. I changed or ignored my reference points because I passionately felt I could create a win.

It was so easy to do. True, I overspent my budget. But, once inside Russia, I discovered that my initial calculations underestimated the costs of starting and maintaining a Russian enterprise. True, I did not acquire a single piece of science within the timeframe I stipulated. But, I identified several promising technologies, including an alluring, light-sensitive compound that reduced the size of cancer tumors. I believed that I could own these technologies if I just had a little more time. True, the political, legal, and commercial environments in Russia impeded the advance of free marketeering. But, I believed that the flow of world history would accelerate Russia's transformation.

On that train, I absolutely believed I was oh, so close to winning. I could taste it. I abandoned my initial, rationally developed measurement criteria in favor of revised reference points created on the fly. My emotions trumped my brain. I lost touch with reality.

You will know if you are losing and if you have lost if you judge yourself by using consistent, factually grounded, measurement criteria. These reference points are more reliable when developed with forethought rather than in response to real time changes during your activities. Yes, of course, some experiences genuinely require adjustments to measurement criteria mid-stream. But, these situations are exceptions, not the norm. Mid-loss is not the time to confuse intellectual flexibility with self-honesty. Strip emotion and hope from your measurement process and think dispassionately before sacrificing pre-established, objective standards of judgment.

Measurements signal when you are losing and, ultimately, when you have lost. Ideally, measurements convince you of the loss in real time, precisely at the time when the loss occurs. A basketball game, for example, is measured in terms of points scored and time elapsed. When the final buzzer sounds and you are two points behind, the game is over. You lost. The measurements are unassailable – no time left and not enough points on the board. You hear the buzzer. You see the scoreboard. In real time, you know you lost.

Events that strike your senses of sight or hearing or touch invite easy, accurate, and immediate measurement. An example: Your house burns down. You arrive on scene and see the charred walls and beams. You suffered a loss. You know it immediately when you see it. Another example: While rebuilding your house, you misfire a hammer blow and smash your thumb. You hurt immediately. You don't need an x-ray to confirm your loss. You, and the rest of the neighborhood, know that you lost.

When the situation is more abstract, devising and using precise measurement standards becomes more vexing. A career or health-related loss is more abstract than a loss in a sporting contest. Yet, you certainly can come up with fact-based, analytical measurements to reference your position in these situations. Suffering a loss in an interpersonal relationship is even more abstract. How do you measure the moment when the loss of your marriage occurs? Is it when your husband comes home drunk for the tenth time? Philanders the fifth time? Physically abuses you the first time? You feel the pain as surely as you do after hitting your thumb with a hammer. But, measuring the moment of loss seems so elusive, almost inhumane. How do you calibrate and adhere to objective criteria while withstanding the subjective vestiges of desire or love? What reliable standard should you use? When do you truly suffer the loss?

Consider this true example: A bright, caring, vivacious woman married an insipid, rude, unattractive man. Aside from some common professional activities, their interests rarely overlapped. For reasons still mysterious to me, she loved and doted on this fellow. In return, he often demeaned her with sarcasm and initiated few acts of tenderness. After ten years of marriage, and quite by accident, she discovered that her husband was involved in a long-running affair. Further investigation revealed a string of lies. She discovered that her husband had married at least twice and had sired at least two children by someone else. A horror story.

The woman instructed her lawyers to file for divorce. Fearing a violent confrontation at home, she had the papers served to her husband while he was out of town on a business trip. On that day, she also changed the locks on the doors of the house so that he could not re-enter.

Whatever the woman's objective measurements were, she clearly understood that she had suffered a big loss. Her marriage was over, her love spurned, her husband a vulgar sham. Yet on the afternoon of his return flight, only a day after changing the locks on her doors and suing him for divorce, she looked up from her cup of coffee and in all seriousness unleashed this stunner: "Do you think I should pick him up at the airport?"

Big interpersonal losses are cruelly disorienting. They shake your faith in the people you most loved or trusted. Strong emotions and intense feelings tempt you to rationalize that this type of loss is in some way different from all other losses. It is not. A loss of a relationship is exactly the same as any other loss.

To win after a big interpersonal loss, you still must recognize the loss and know when it occurs. Measure the loss of a relationship by using and adhering to objective standards. No magic formula exists to create these objective criteria. I can't tell you – and no one else can – if, by your standards, it's OK for your spouse to sleep with another person. You decide. You decide if once is one too many. You decide if your relationship deserves a second chance or a third or a fiftieth. Read no sermon here. I'm speaking dispassionately, only about objective measurements, only about how and when to recognize a loss. You define your measurement standards. Then, shield them from emotions past.

Recognizing the loss of a relationship severely tests your self-honesty. But, pretending or rationalizing that you have not suffered an interpersonal loss prevents you from recognizing the loss and stymies your ability to get back up. Through the pain, rely on your objective measurement standards and recognize the loss of a relationship exactly when the loss occurs.

Suffering a big loss, any type of big loss, crushes you. You can barely breathe at that moment of recognition, that instant when your mind absorbs the defeat. You are alone, frustrated, angry, and overwhelmed by the colossus. You wonder how you can ever recover. But, you already know how to win after losing. You've won after smaller losses without even thinking about it. But, now think about this:

✶ To create a win after suffering a big loss, you must define precisely what you lost.

Exaggeration undermines recovery from a loss. When you suffer a big loss, your mind exaggerates plenty. Amid the emotional carnage, you imagine yourself under a forty-ton boulder or at the bottom of a thousand-foot chasm or outnumbered by an attacking horde. Whatever the imagery, you see yourself alone against the world, crippled by the enormity of the burden you bear, paralyzed by the mammoth obstacle in your path.

Resist exaggeration. Just as you objectively determined when you lost, you must summon your self-honesty to define what you lost. An example: You lost your job. Perhaps it was a wonderful job, the job of your dreams. But, it was one job. You did not lose your ability to earn a living or get another job, perhaps a better one.

A tougher, true example: I worked with an analytically brilliant fellow who suffered from a congenital eye disease. For five years, he slowly and knowingly went blind. He angrily fought it every step of the way. He refused to stop driving until he demolished his car. Refused to buy a cane until he fell down a flight of stairs. Refused to retire until he could not tolerate the embarrassment of performing ineffectively.

Completely sightless, he left his job and reconfigured his life. He spent more time with his children and his wife. He worked with organizations assisting the blind. He used voice-activated computer devices and started a small, now growing, consultancy. He lost his sight, an unquestionably irreplaceable loss. Yet, he did not lose his ability to sense the world acutely and participate with passion.

Understand, I'm not minimizing the magnitude of a big loss. But, every big loss is finite. And that's really my point. However huge your loss, it has boundaries. Find those boundaries. Define your loss so that you can isolate it. Bound your loss so that you can see beyond it. Your next win will not undo your loss. Your next win will occur beyond the horizon of your loss.

Losing is not a sin. Then, why do you feel so soiled after suffering a big loss? Why do you curse yourself and demand penance? Why do you doubt your judgment and second-guess the simplest of decisions? Why do you abhor living inside yourself? Why do you condemn yourself to that corner of hell reserved for losers?

There is no corner in hell reserved for losers. Losing requires no admission of guilt, only recognition of fact. Losing requires no self-flagellation, no penance. Suffering a big loss neither damns you nor demands that you relinquish your self-esteem.

To create a win after suffering a big loss, you must respect yourself.

Losing attacks you in the mirror. The truth is, you feel horrible after a big loss because you have let yourself down. Self-disappointment obliterates self-confidence, self-trust, and ultimately, self-respect. Regardless of the consequences of the loss, regardless of the damage you may have caused to others, you feel inconsolably terrible primarily because you have disappointed yourself. And worse, you are spectacularly afraid that your now proven incompetence and ineptitude will rain losses on you forevermore. Nonsense.

To rebuild your self-respect, you must recognize why you lost.

Do you think that understanding why you lost will prevent you from future losses? Maybe, but don't bet on it. Sure, learn from your loss. If you encounter and recognize the same pattern of circumstances again, you may be able to avert an oncoming defeat. But, how probable is that? Unfortunately, the odds are much greater that you will never see that exact fact pattern again. Something, perhaps subtly important, will be different. Losses occur in an infinite variety. Most likely, each of your losses will be unique.

Understanding why you lost is important for a more practical reason. You need to understand why you lost so that you can stop beating yourself up. Recognizing why you lost reveals your true role in the loss. You will regain your self-esteem by understanding your contribution to the loss and the contribution of other factors. This time, isolate and bound your *responsibility* for the loss. Again, summon your self-honesty. Take fair, but finite, blame for the loss.

Recapturing your self-respect after suffering a big loss occurs when you understand why you lost and when you accurately define your responsibility for the loss. Understanding *why* you lost requires that you recognize the *causes* of your loss. Defining your *responsibility* for a loss requires that you recognize the extent that you could *control* the causes of the loss.

All losses derive from at least one of three causes:

1. Model Error
2. Execution Failure
3. Random Misfortune

Almost always, more than one of these causes combine to produce a big loss. You can control Model Error and

Execution Failure to some degree. Random Misfortune is totally beyond your control.

Model Error means that your prediction of events differs significantly from the actual occurrence of events. Simply put, you believe something is going to happen and it does not. You live your life based on an ever-changing set of assumptions. You make and revise these assumptions constantly. You use these assumptions to construct a model of events likely to occur. An example: You live on the twentieth floor of an apartment building. Every morning, you kiss your spouse good-bye, exit your front door, walk down the hall, stand in front of a set of closed, sliding doors, push a button on the wall to summon the elevator, and begin reading your newspaper. When those doors slide open, you do not glance up from the news article. Instead, you instinctively enter the doorway. You assume, based on past experience, the elevator is indeed there. Suppose it's not? You make an egregious Model Error and suffer a plummeting loss.

Many Model Errors result from inadvertent actions based on faith in seemingly insignificant assumptions. You subconsciously believe that your world today will follow the same patterns as your world of every yesterday. You are comfortable with assumptions that seem so reliably certain. Model Errors beget poor judgment.

Not all Model Errors result from carelessness. Return with me to Russia again. My model for my success in the former Soviet Union included the assumption that the United States would sponsor a "Marshall Plan" to boost Russia's transformation. I thought about this in great detail and received educated counsel from respected pundits. But, in the end, my assumption proved grossly wrong. Events did not turn out the way I predicted. Neither the government nor the economy of Russia was as stable as I assumed. No "Marshall Plan" appeared. This

Model Error was a critical cause of my venture's failure.

Execution Failure means that imperfections or mistakes in your actions prevent you from winning. Starkly stated, flaws in your performance cause you to lose. Execution Failures can occur even if you try your best. Suppose, for example, you are a marathon runner. You train hard, understand the race course, plan your strategy superbly, run the best time of your life – and still lose to a faster marathoner. This is Execution Failure, unfortunate but true. You lost for no reason other than you could not move your legs fast enough to beat the first place finisher. You made no mistakes. You tried your best. You performed as well as you could. You simply failed to perform well enough to win.

Clearly, by not winning the race, you suffered a loss, perhaps with severe consequences. Perhaps the loss caused you to miss qualifying for the Olympic Team, squelching a lifelong dream. No question, this is a big loss. But, how should you react? Anger? Disappointment? Frustration? Sadness? Of course. But, you made no mistakes. You ran your best. Recognize the loss and recognize that you could do nothing to avert the loss. Take responsibility for the loss with your self-respect completely intact.

But, most Execution Failures occur when you do make a mistake. Certainly, you don't intend to err. But, you do and your flawed performance causes you to lose. Suppose, for example, you finish second in the marathon because you ate squid rather than pasta on the night before the race. Worse, imagine that you are a pilot who lands at the wrong airport, a surgeon who amputates the healthy leg, or a mother too distracted to hear her drowning toddler's cries for help.

Accepting why you lost when you are unquestionably at fault is excruciatingly difficult. The inescapable truth is that you could and should have performed better. But, you did not. You made a mistake. Your mistake produced the loss, perhaps a gigantic loss. What else could so effectively shatter your self-respect?

It's easy to respond to Execution Failure with self-delusion. But, resist the temptation to search for someone or something else to blame. Instead, admit to yourself that you made a mistake. Acknowledge the truth, no matter how horrible. Your error caused the loss.

Without this admission, you lie to yourself. This is no white lie of convenience. It's a whopper and it's dangerous. The lie torments you because it prevents you from bounding the loss. And, the lie further decays your self-respect. Self-respect, above all, requires self-honesty.

✳ To rebuild your self-respect after a self-inflicted Execution Failure, you must accept undeniable and sole responsibility for the loss.

Random Misfortune means that bad luck causes you to suffer a loss. Recognize that uncontrollable mischance may cause you to lose. Surprised? Well, the truth is: "Wildcards" sprinkle your life. Some losses occur for reasons you cannot control. These are genuine losses, sometimes with enormous consequences. But, your role in losing is completely passive. You did not cause the loss. You are not responsible for the loss. You should not feel guilty for suffering the loss. Your self-respect should never waver.

Health-related losses frequently derive from Random

Misfortune. Recall my blind acquaintance. His loss occurred only because of his genetics. Terrible luck.

Losing makes you feel unlucky and invites you to feel victimized. But, I urge you to resist the convenience of claiming Random Misfortune as truly the cause of your loss. Be scrupulously honest. Before relieving yourself of responsibility, re-examine the loss acutely for any hint of Model Error or Execution Failure.

The bathtub in my Soviet-era apartment shared a swiveled spigot with my kitchen sink. This curious architectural detail enabled me to wash myself simultaneously with my dinner dishes. I tried this only once, but aborted immediately when the clanking plumbing signaled the demise of all hot water, perhaps for days. As I rinsed and dried, I thought about my Russian colleagues – top notch research scientists – who frequently went home to cold pipes.

These hard-workers lost big. For many, lifetimes of research, intellectual fulfillment, and family security disintegrated along with their oppressive government. Isolated in academic and military cubbyholes, they never believed that they were losing. And when the enormity of the collapse became incontrovertibly clear, they neither asked nor fully understood why they lost.

On my last day in Russia, at Moscow's airport, I saw the same silent acquiescence in the downcast eyes of the Russian grandmothers who cleaned the interior of my Delta jet. Blue, front-buttoned dresses and bulky gray cardigans stretched over their broad backs and heavy chests. They carried brooms made from twigs and plastic sacks filled with trash. Stoically, they searched the pockets in every seat-back for the fringe benefits of their job, wayward pieces of airline tableware and left-behind bits of foil wrapped chocolate.

My Russian venture was a gigantic bust. The loss emptied my pockets, stole my time, and most cruelly, stripped my self-respect. It dismantled my mental and emotional gyroscope, then dared me to rediscover my brain, my heart, and ultimately, my will to recover. Retreating westward above the Atlantic, I gazed numbly at the white dappled azure and let the sunshine bake me to sleep. When I awoke, I wondered if the stunned scientists, weary cleaning ladies, and I were groping for the same elusive truths.

Recognizing your loss is complex. It requires an open and inquisitive mind. It requires that you ask yourself difficult questions and honestly answer. It requires your proactive, not passive, attention. How well you understand yourself is at the heart of winning smart after losing big. Your self-respect is essential for you to create your next victory. To earn it, carefully understand when you lost, what you lost, and why you lost.

Did this Chapter stimulate you? Share your specific thoughts, questions, and experiences with other readers of **WINNING SMART** AFTER LOSING BIG by logging onto www.robstearns.com. Then, go to the Forum page, select "Chapter Four: Recognize Your Loss" from the Forum List, and join the discussion.

CHAPTER FIVE
YOUR MIND MENDS
YOUR HEART

The most remarkable letter I ever received was from a group of people I did not know. They invited me here, to an attic atop an abused building in Brooklyn. The room is narrow, with a high ceiling and peeling brown walls. Fine grit covers the floorboards. I am sitting on a straight-backed, oak chair. When I lean back and pull my elbows off the matching table, sticky layers of old varnish grab my shirtsleeves. Behind me, a corroded faucet drips into a cast iron sink, deep and rusty white. Sunlight diffuses into the room through wire mesh, through smears of grime and pigeon droppings, through cracked glass windows. The air smells warm and thick and sweet, a blanket of chocolate.

Across the table from me sits the teacher who funded and built this makeshift fudge factory under the eaves of this inner city high school. He is fortyish, with sandy hair and ruddy face, a big man about to explode out of his undersized, plaid blazer. His eyes brighten blue while he explains fudge production with the enthusiasm of a world explorer. He uses the factory to teach practical lessons about hygiene, mathematics, and teamwork to special education students. Together, they manufacture and sell chocolate candy after the regular school day ends.

We chew on warm fudge with walnuts while I get an

education. Here's what I hear: The city's education budget provides no money for the fudge factory. Despite repeated petitioning, the teacher still awaits official authorization for the school janitor to fix the sink. Despite several years of cajoling, he cannot persuade the janitor to fix it without the official OK. He knows that he cannot save many of his students from short or troubled lives. He enjoys the process of trying.

Here's what I learn: This teacher loves his job and is a devoted educator. His day essentially consists of a stream of losses, occasionally interrupted by a win. He perceives losing and winning differently than I do. He is motivated differently, too. I could not get out of bed each morning and do his job with his sense of upbeat passion while knowing the long, long odds against winning.

Here's what I wonder: How similarly do you and I perceive losing and winning? Can we adjust these perceptions to improve our odds of winning after losing?

Perception consists of thinking and feeling. I'm sure that comprehensive explanations exist to differentiate these two phenomena. But, for me, it's pretty simple. Your mind thinks. Concentrate hard enough on thinking and you actually become aware of something going on inside your head. Feelings are located somewhere else. Your innards – the pit of your stomach, the depth of your heart – feel. Falling in love is feeling. Deciding to rotate the tires is thinking.

Thinking is a rational process that you can control. You can start thinking and stop, accelerate your thinking and slow it down. Sometimes your thoughts may be jumbled. But, most of the time you can decide what to think about and in what sequence. You can think concretely or in the abstract about the past, present, and future. Frequently, external stimuli trigger thoughts. Just as often, your mind starts thinking unprovoked by outside events.

In contrast, feeling is almost always an emotional response that arrives uninvited and unsorted. You can feel an extraordinary range of emotions. They come in whispers and roars, fleeting and lasting. The smell of baking pies, a familiar melody, a flash of the color red, a caress on the cheek – physical sensations often conjure feelings. Feelings frequently derive from external occurrences. But, a memory or an association may produce strong feelings also. Even certain words can trigger feelings. Here, I'll say one and I bet you feel something. Puppies.

After a big loss, you and I feel the same tidal waves of horrible sensations. That lump in your throat is a feeling. That fear of facing tomorrow is a feeling. That helpless despair, inconsolable grief, crushing pressure, heavy fatigue – all feelings. These feelings stab your nerves during daylight and bleed tranquility from you at night. Time passes so slowly. Nothing seems more urgent than the need to cure the pain and compression that you feel. And, that's why this is so hard to believe:

How you *think* about losing and winning

is more important than

how you *feel* about losing and winning.

Read the next paragraph carefully. Read it several times so that it sinks in. It is the toughest paragraph to understand in this book. But, when you absorb it, you will realize that the magic is in *your* mind, not mine.

Feelings do not cause you to win or lose. Only actions produce victories or defeats. How you think determines how you act. But powerful feelings, instantaneously or over time, can influence how you think. You cannot trust powerful feelings to help you win. True, they may motivate you. But, they may equally lead you astray. Your mind is strong enough to recognize and think about your feelings. But, you must consciously force your mind to think about how you feel. If you understand how you feel, you can manage your feelings. Managing your feelings allows rational thinking to drive your actions. Rational thinking produces actions that enhance your odds of winning.

⚔ Understanding and managing
your emotions
after a major loss
is a win.

Rational thinking may or may not make you feel good. In fact, winning may not always make you feel completely good. After all, how wonderful do you really feel after winning an argument with your spouse? Boxing champions, after defeating their mentors or heroes, frequently recall feeling sad during the bouts and afterwards. Winning is not the same as feeling good. Winning after losing provides no guarantee that you will feel better about the loss. But, winning after losing will make you feel better about yourself.

To win after a major loss, you must control enormous surges of feelings with conscious thought and a potent dose of self-honesty. Managing your feelings is essential for you to recognize the loss and accurately assign responsibility for it. No one seems immune to the emotional cascades that accompany a big defeat. Sometimes, even supposed human behavior experts fail to re-establish the vital balance between thinking and feeling.

Consider the long lasting tremor of love and sexual attraction in this true example: I recently visited a well-known psychiatrist. The session involved no personal therapy, probably much to the disappointment of many who know me well. Rather, at the suggestion of a mutual friend, the doctor met with me to discuss losing and winning. We traded perspectives for a half an hour or so. Then, I asked the psychiatrist to talk about his greatest loss.

The doctor leaned back in his swivel chair, eyes focused on me and then far away. He paused, perhaps musing on the odd role reversal and wondering whether he should confide in a stranger. I waited until he softly spoke, his voice righteous and sad.

The psychiatrist told me that, years ago, he fell in love with a female patient. At the time, he was treating her for self-destructive behavior. Their passionate affair spanned several years. When it cooled, the patient ended her medical relationship with him. Their secret outlived the patient, who died by her own hand a decade later.

Close to twenty years after the affair, the psychiatrist's life erupted. A chance reading of the patient's private writings by a curious journalist brought the tryst to daylight. The writer exposed the affair in a broadly circulated publication. You can predict the rest. Hospitals stripped the psychiatrist of professional privileges. His thriving practice evaporated. His wife filed for divorce. In short order, a complete professional and family meltdown. Big, big losses.

But, can you predict this renowned psychiatrist's perception of what happened? As he described the affair to me, the doctor stated, several times, that he knew that he had "crossed the line" of unprofessional behavior. Yet, he asserted that his colleagues and family judged him too severely. He never quite admitted to me or to himself that his conduct was inexcusably improper. Instead, still captured in a vortex of feelings, he looked at me and rationalized his behavior with this wowser: "You know, she never attempted suicide while we were involved."

After a major loss, feeling overpowers thinking. And, that imbalance impedes winning. Feelings that engulf you after losing are aftershocks of the loss itself – unalterable history continuing to haunt you in the present. These hyper-strong emotions suck you backward in time – precisely in the wrong direction – and mire you in the past. You replay your loss in an attempt to improve how you feel. But, the replay draws you into a tortured loop. From your current plight, you review events leading up to the loss, ponder what you might have done to avoid the loss, wonder why you did not prevent the loss, and live again the moment of the loss. That's precisely your path if you complete the outermost circuit of the Replay Loops, shown below, in Exhibit 3.

Exhibit 3: Replay Loops

No surprise that, rather than feeling liberated, you feel worse. Run the replay again and you feel even more terrible. That's why, when you start to replay the loss, you should try to abbreviate the circuit. At first, try to reduce it to a partial loop. Every time your replay begins, try to cut the arc shorter and shorter. Ultimately, when the replay launches, recognize what's happening, then instantly stop the loop at its start.

Replays lure you with false hopes, a chimera of "what ifs." They cannot subdue the awful feelings that shackle you to a loss. In fact, replays aggravate your emotional imbalance. They force you to face passively backwards to witness an irreversible, past defeat. Winning requires the exact opposite. Winning demands your active mental participation. Winning stretches, uncharted, ahead of you.

To turn away from the past and face forward, you must consciously elevate thinking above feeling.

I'm not suggesting that you should ignore your feelings after a big loss. You cannot avoid them and you should not try. Experience them deeply, without shame. Grieve. Feel terrible. But, wallowing in pure emotion glues you to an unchangeable yesterday. While there is absolutely nothing wrong with feeling awful after a big loss, simply feeling awful will neither undo the loss nor create your next win. To face forward, understand and explore your emotions. Then, manage your feelings with your mind. Winning after losing requires thinking.

Although you and I share similar emotions after losing,

we probably think about our individual losses differently. For example, our thinking about the size of a loss may vary. We may define "big loss" differently. What may be a huge defeat for me may be only a minor setback for you. What causes me great pain may hardly bother you at all.

Similarly, our thinking about the frequency of losing may vary. We may define "losing often" differently. For me, a single loss during a week may deliver a stunning emotional jolt. You, on the other hand, may withstand a battering of defeats every day and feel just fine.

Understanding how you think about "losing big" and "losing often" is important. Knowing how your own mind perceives the size and frequency of a loss empowers you to put your loss into a personal perspective. You need this mental framework as a starting point for your mind to grasp and manage your feelings.

I speak with many people about losing and winning. While I claim no statistical sophistication, I do notice patterns. I believe you feel losing and winning with predictable consistency. Think about it. You know how losing and winning make you feel. Your genetics, personality, upbringing, education, livelihood, and no doubt other factors contribute to this emotional predictability. We could spend a long time theorizing about these underlying causes.

But, my point is purely pragmatic: You will recover from a big loss more easily if you can stabilize and manage your feelings. By consciously recognizing your own emotional pattern, you again elevate thinking above feeling. Your mind frames your emotional perspective. You proactively think more, reactively feel less.

After a loss or a win, most people's feelings fit into one of three patterns: Hyper-High, Hyper-Low, or Balanced. Take a look at the Intensity Arcs illustrated on the next page in Exhibit 4.

Exhibit 4: Intensity Arcs

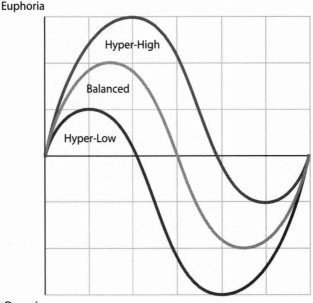

Euphoria

Hyper-High

Balanced

Hyper-Low

Despair

Each of the curves represents the intensity of a different individual's feelings after a loss or win of the same size, or a series of losses or wins of the same frequency. Do you feel winning more powerfully than you feel losing? Then, your feelings follow the arcs shown as Hyper-High. Or, are you the exact opposite? Do you feel losing more intensely than winning? If so, your emotions trace the Hyper-Low arcs. Or, do you feel losing and winning with about the same force? Then, your feelings resemble the Balanced arcs.

Think about how you consistently feel when you win or lose. I bet you already see a familiar pattern in your own emotions. You're fitting yourself onto one of the arcs right now, aren't you? Are you Hyper-High, Hyper-Low, or Balanced?

ROB STEARNS | 59

Of course, the arcs are just tools. They make you think. They encourage your mind to examine how you feel highs and lows. They elevate thinking above feeling. Your arc provides a reference, a mental reminder of your proclivity to feel distress or euphoria. And after a major loss, when you are under emotional siege, you need this engagement of your mind to recognize and manage your feelings.

The three patterns fascinate me because they illustrate why you and I tolerate losing differently. Recall, for example, the terrific teacher in the fudge factory, bombarded by a steady rain of losses. Or, consider a devoted minister, every Sunday preaching to a yawning flock of never-to-be-saved souls. Teachers and ministers generally are Hyper-Highs. They feel winning more intensely than losing. They feel joy in even small wins and are relatively impervious to repeated losses. In fact, they expect to lose more than they win. They rarely count losses and wins or judge themselves by a win/loss ratio. Instead, Hyper-Highs define victory in terms of "making a difference." Talk to a clergyman about winning and losing and you will eventually hear words that mean "any win is better than none."

Hyper-Highs often define losing and winning narrowly. They mentally confine losses and wins to only situations that are within their control. People on the frontlines of disaster and crime prevention frequently buffer their daily horrors and frustrations with this mental outlook.

A police officer describing her biggest loss provided me with this true illustration: For years, she worked closely with teenagers in street gangs to reduce violence in a western city. She knew many gang members and developed tenuous, but reciprocal, bonds of trust. One rainy morning, while patrolling a tough neighborhood, she drove past two female gang members walking towards their high school. She knew the girls and stopped to offer them a ride. They gladly accepted, rode with her for several minutes, politely held her up at knifepoint, and stole her police car. Marooned and chagrinned, she used her cell phone to alert the police station and arrange for her extrication. For a month afterwards, she received merciless ribbing by her fellow officers that ended only when the next bonehead event inevitably supplanted hers.

Wouldn't you think that this policewoman would relate a more tragic loss? Isn't this where we should hear stomach turning details about the stabbing murder of a promising youth, the varsity track star whose life's blood oozed out in front of his mother as he crawled up his front stoop? The officer spoke to the point. "I do the best I can. But, I can't control everything that goes on in the streets. I can't control the shootings and the stabbings. Yes, the violence bothers me. But, I only measure losses and wins in the context of events that I can control. I should have prevented the theft of my vehicle."

Most of the business people and attorneys that I know would not survive as inner city teachers or police officers. They are Hyper-Lows. They intellectually understand the staccato of losing and winning in their lives. But with consistent irrationality, most expect to win all of the time. They are stunned when they lose and feel extraordinarily bad. They judge themselves and are judged by others explicitly by the number and the frequency of their wins.

Speak with a Wall Streeter or read a corporate titan's memoirs. Their words often convey hatred for losing and disdain for people who lose. A successful litigator acknowledged the irrationality to me this way: "Any lawyer that wins all of the time is avoiding the tough cases. I enjoy arguing the tough ones. And, I truly believe that I can win each of them when I am on trial. Losing always comes as an unpleasant surprise."

Hyper-Lows, many business people for example, are frequently highly competitive. They consider themselves athletes playing high stakes games. But most real athletes are not Hyper-Low. Professional athletes are typically Balanced. For sure, they feel losing intensely. Look in the eyes of the defeated players on the bench as the final seconds of a championship game tick away if you need tears as proof. And yes, outsiders judge athletes by the number and frequency of their losses and wins. But most athletes, in contrast, measure themselves by the quality of their performance. They acknowledge personal Execution Failure and the vexing role of Random Misfortune. But, they also understand their loss is finite and that the condition of losing is temporal. Athletes know and believe that tomorrow offers the chance to win again. Not the same game. Perhaps not with the same consequences. But, at least a fresh opportunity to win anew.

Almost always, athletes see positive elements buried within a loss. Come into the locker rooms with me. After discussing a costly errant tee shot, a professional golfer recounts a long putt snaking into the hole. After losing a five hundred mile race by tenths of a second, a race car driver remarks on the efficiency of his pit crew. After giving up the winning run, a relief pitcher admits, "I just didn't have my best stuff, *today*." At first, this seems to be the palaver of good sportsmanship. But, it's more than that. It's a peek into Balanced athletes' minds when they elevate thinking above feeling. An owner of a major league baseball team, once a pretty fair ballplayer himself, succinctly summarized the athlete's perspective to me: "Athletes are in the business of losing and winning. They know that playing a game is a calculated risk. They want to win all of the time, but they know they will not. Athletes understand that losing is a part of winning."

Here's an interesting question: Does any one of these patterns – Hyper-High, Hyper-Low, or Balanced – improve your odds of winning after losing? The surprising answer is no. Here's why: You win with your mind, not with your heart. Sure, you may feel better after losing if you are Balanced rather than Hyper-Low. But, what you feel and how intensely you feel have very little to do with actually creating your next win. You can win when you are crestfallen, euphoric, sedate, or lava hot mad. Try to visualize any mix of your feelings on the Emotion Map, shown below, in Exhibit 5.

Exhibit 5: Emotion Map

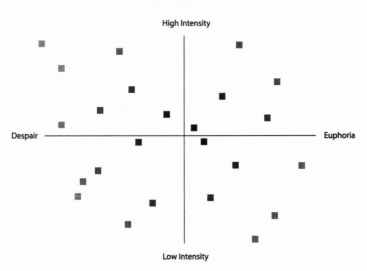

Here's a truth: No point on this map either guarantees you a win or improves your odds of winning.

Winning requires no emotional constant.

After suffering a big loss, spend not an iota of energy

trying to revamp your own emotional pattern. That's a long term, long odds project. Instead, use your mind to acknowledge your feelings. Put the intensity of your emotions into personal perspective. Then, as quickly as you can, force your mind to start thinking about creating your next win.

Let's also debunk a particularly sophomoric adage: "Time heals all wounds." Ridiculous. And, possibly harmful if you believe it after suffering a big loss. Time is not an omnipotent cure-all. Need convincing? Think about an irreplaceable loss that you suffered years ago. Think about the death of your parent or child, the crushing of a lifelong dream, or the betrayal of your love. Still hurt? You bet.

Yet, right after re-experiencing the pain of an ancient loss, your mind takes over, doesn't it? Perhaps a comforting memory dilutes the anguish. Or, perhaps the knowledge of a subsequent win calms the anger. Time puts distance between you and a loss. This distance helps your mind put your loss into perspective. Time gives you the chance to think about winning after losing.

But, time is a luxury. You can't count on having it when you need it. And, it's an odd ally. Too much time may actually dilute your sense of urgency and stall your effort to get back up. Time is not a universal salve. After a loss, the elapse of time permits you to think. But, time is not a substitute for thinking.

Losing is lonely – a curiosity, since everyone loses. But, the isolation is real. Soon after suffering a major loss, you understand why: No one is going to create your next win for you. You must rely on yourself to win again. More specifically, you must rely on your mind to manage your emotions and guide your actions. Self-reliance requires that you differentiate between feeling and thinking. Self-reliance demands that you trust your judgment. Self-reliance really means that you use your mind to mend your heart.

———

Climb the stairs to the attic fudge factory with me one more time. Meet a dozen special education students, measuring and mixing sugar and giggles. Few can read at their grade level. Many have learning disabilities. Most come to school craving safety from the streets and often, from home. These boys and girls feel losing every day. But, they think about winning, too. They understand. They wrote the letter inviting me to meet their teacher.

Did this Chapter stimulate you? Share your specific thoughts, questions, and experiences with other readers of **WINNING SMART** AFTER LOSING BIG by logging onto www.robstearns.com. Then, go to the Forum page, select "Chapter Five: Your Mind Mends Your Heart" from the Forum List, and join the discussion.

CHAPTER SIX
LET THE OUTSIDE IN

I'm standing in the bedroom doorway, studying my father. The lamp on his nightstand glows yellow and warm on a cold autumn night. Two mashed pillows and a rumpled quilt surrendered moments before I arrived and mostly lie tangled on the floor. He is perched upright on the far side of the bed, his back facing me. He sits still, with his arms at each side, hands grasping the mattress edge for support. He doesn't sense my presence.

His mussed hair stands up on both sides of his head. I stare at the pink and white tumor protruding from his right temple and follow the line of his skinny neck down to the collar of his blue, long sleeved, pajamas. The fabric, now several sizes too large, blouses around his torso. His bony pointed shoulders make little bumps in the silk, as if the shirt is worn by a clothes hanger with a head rather than by a man.

I know that he is in great pain. When he inhales, he holds each breath for a moment, then slowly releases. I have no idea what he is thinking as he sits there, gazing at his bureau, five years into the battle and less than a month from his dying day. He is losing everything and he surely knows it.

And, as I stand in the doorway, I know that I am losing, too. At that moment, I actually wish for him to die soon, relieved of the pain, free of the torture that comes with the truth when no happy ending awaits.

Bearing a tray of tea and toast, I cough and he hears me. He looks over his shoulder, leans back on one arm, and gamely stifles a wince. He smiles, but his eyes do not.

"How are you feeling?" I ask.

"OK. How are you doing?"

"OK."

Losing makes liars of us all. We lie to ourselves first. But, you already understand the importance of self-honesty. Recognizing your loss requires that you tell yourself the truth. Always. Mending your heart with your mind requires that you tell yourself the truth. Always.

Unfortunately, the truth you tell yourself is not the whole truth to tell. Here's why: You never lose in a total vacuum. Yes, losing is lonely and isolating. But, your loss always affects other people. Unwittingly, when you lose, you have partners. They, too, have a claim on the truth.

Partners? Who are these people? Family, friends, acquaintances, and strangers – all on scene to witness your loss and interact with you afterwards. Some view your loss up close and are fouled by the consequences. Others see your collapse from afar and mightily appreciate their distance. Fans, detractors, impartial bystanders – all of these people know that you are down, vulnerable, and at your worst. When we lose big, we instinctively lie to every one of them.

What's the lie? Simple. The lie is: "I'm OK."

But the truth is, when you suffer a major loss, you're not OK. You're emotionally shell shocked. Mentally frazzled. Physically drained. You're not even close to OK. And you know you're not, even as you reflexively utter the lie.

Still, "I'm OK" seems pretty harmless as lies go. It's easy to understand. After suffering a major loss, you curtain the truth to conceal your weaknesses from other people. You want no prying eyes to probe the flawed nakedness of your defeat. In fact, the lie appears downright gallant. You shade the truth to spare other people from hefting your burdens.

This is very seductive logic because it may be correct. It may explain exactly why you lie, why you say "I'm OK" when you're obviously not. Yes, you want to preserve your dignity. Yes, you hate to shovel your woes onto other people. But if you believe this comfortable rationale, you give yourself compelling, or at least convenient, reasons to continue lying about your loss. And, you should stop. Here's why:

To win after suffering a major loss, you need the help of other people.

Not you? Well, compare the words with the actions of a fellow naysayer. Recently, I had a telling conversation with a highly principled, strong-minded, legislator. During the past thirty years, he suffered several big losses, including the death of his father, the dissolution of his marriage, and the loss of his elected office. I asked him to talk about the people who provided help after his defeats. Without pause, he said, "No one helped me. And, I didn't ask for anyone for help. I just put my head down and bulled my way through."

Amazing. How did he do that?

He joined the Marines. After the death of his father, he enlisted. During the disintegration of his marriage, he volunteered for another tour of duty overseas. And, after the tough electoral defeat, he again returned to serve the military.

Now, think about what he really did. He looked for and found help. He joined the Marine *Corps*, a body of people bonded together by the motto *Semper Fidelis*, translated "Always Faithful." Always faithful to your country. Always faithful to your fellow Marines. And vitally important, your fellow Marines always faithful *to you*. He received help from people explicitly sworn to provide help.

Everyone, *everyone*, who recovers from a major loss receives help from someone else. This is the absolute common thread that unites all people who win after losing. No one, *no one*, recovers alone. It's so important that you should read it again:

To win after suffering a major loss, you need the help of other people.

Lying about your loss pushes away the people you need to help you. When you say, "I'm OK," people hear, "Keep your distance. I don't need your help." Rebuffed, they withdraw and allow you to struggle alone. That's not what you want. After losing big, you need all the help you can get.

You must honestly acknowledge your loss to other people to obtain their help.

What, then, makes this confession so excruciating? Why do you deny a loss that's so obviously visible to everyone around you? When you need help, why do you hesitate to ask for it and, worse, resist accepting it? What's the real reason why you cough up a bloody "I'm OK?"

Control. You want control over your life. Period. Every losing experience strips you of control. You never wake-up in the morning and think, "Ahh, what a great day to take it on the chin." No, losing starkly illustrates that you cannot control all events all of the time. If you could, you would prevent all of your losses.

Accepting help puts more than your dignity or selflessness at stake. Accepting help makes you dependent, at least partially, on someone other than yourself. You rebel because you equate dependency with subordination, with loss of control. Perhaps cultural conditioning, perhaps human genetics fuels your resistance. Either way, what's clear is that you perceive accepting help from someone else as – another loss.

Absolutely, another loss. You believe that accepting help suppresses your masculinity, your femininity, your individuality, your self-sufficiency. You worry that accepting help carves your face on some imaginary totem pole of losers, a permanent monument to your inferiority. "I'm OK" looks small and sounds innocuous. But, the lie is large and trumpets: "I refuse to surrender my independence."

What a mind-bender. Help from other people seems to dilute your self-reliance. But to recover from a big loss, you certainly need both. How do you reconcile the two? How can you receive help from others and remain independent? Think hard about this Paradox of Self-Reliance:

You are totally self-reliant
only when you can depend on yourself
to select help from other people.

"Select" is the key word. Self-reliance requires your active participation. The fact is, when you accept help, you do surrender some independence. Maybe for a nanosecond, maybe forever. But, here's the cruel truth: With help, you recover. Without help, you don't. So, after suffering a major loss, you must depend on yourself to resolve two intriguing questions. First, how much control over your life should you give up in exchange for help? And second, what is the right help to accept?

The answer to the first question varies. Every big loss forces you to calculate and compare the value of your independence and the value of the help offered to you. Both values fluctuate, depending on the immediacy and the severity of your loss. That's why your willingness to accept help fluctuates, also. Trapped by flames and choked by smoke, you gladly cede all control to the rescuer who drags you to safety. In urgent, survival situations, you welcome help and give up independence with no hesitation. But most losses, even life threatening ones, give you time to mull the trade off.

Losing nibbles at your independence. Losing big devours it. Wary after suffering a major loss, you cherish the scraps. As a result, you repeatedly miscalculate the worth of independence versus the value of help. At the moment when you need help the most, your remaining independence seems too precious to trade. Help, all help, appears to be a bad bargain. Out comes "I'm OK," instead.

Adopting a deflated, but more pragmatic, notion of your independence trues up your reasoning. Try this: Total independence – you as a solo act – is a myth. No one goes it alone and you're not going to be the first. Since conception, you have lived not a single moment of pure independence. During every second of your life, you rely on someone for something.

You know this is true, of course, but you rarely think about it. As your typical day percolates along, uninterrupted by major upset, you live in a pleasant mist of delusional self-sufficiency. But, consider what happens when your community experiences a power failure. At home without lights, you quickly recognize that you need everyday help from others to maintain the normally faultless electrical grid. Ironically, you see your reliance on other people more clearly in the dark.

And, that's my point. Your dependence on other people does not change solely because you lose. Mainly, your awareness changes. You rely on other people to help you all of the time. But, you notice your dependence on their help more acutely during a crisis. Sure, when you lose big, you may need more help or faster help or different help. But, accepting help when you win and then rejecting help when you lose just makes no sense. When your lamps shine brightly, you rely completely on other people to keep the current flowing. During a power outage, do you abandon their help, grab a ladder and a roll of duct tape, and climb a high-tension tower to make the repair yourself?

Independence is not synonymous with isolation. Independence is not code for "me against the universe." Independence has nothing to do with spurning all help. Independence in a highly inter-dependent real world is simply the unfettered use of your mind to make choices.

So, stop lying when you lose. "I'm OK" impedes your

next win. You don't need this fiction to preserve your independence. In fact, you don't need to ration your independence at all. You never run out. You have an infinite supply.

✦ You create independence by using it.

After suffering a major loss, waste no time determining if you need help. You do. Expend no energy debating whether you should trade some of your independence. You should. Focus your thinking, instead, on the second question: What's the right help to take?

Selecting the right help requires you to take charge. I can't tell you exactly what help to choose. The right help depends entirely on the specifics of your loss. But, you improve your odds of getting the right help when you ask for it intelligently.

It's tempting to ask for plenty of imaginative assistance. But unfortunately, the people you approach for help are usually wrestling with their own problems. They can allocate only modest amounts of time and effort to resolving yours. They are not looking for open-ended or mushy assignments.

So, help people help you. Define your requests for help precisely. Be finite. Specify what help is most important to you. Frame each request as a straightforward, action step. Be reasonable. Create requests that people can honor without incurring embarrassment or much risk. Ask for help that people can realistically deliver, given their capabilities and resources.

Do not dawdle. You need help quickly after losing big. Help is rarely plentiful enough. And, offers of help frequently evaporate when ignored. Most importantly, avoid the temptation to wait for a better offer. You're drowning. If someone throws you a bowling ball, of course let it go. But, if someone tosses you a life vest, don't argue about the color or the size. Grab it and put it on. The right help is not necessarily the best help. The right help is often the *only* help available to you.

Selecting the right help is not a matter of fine-tuning. You're choosing between bowling balls and life vests. Dizzy in the funk of a major loss, you still know the difference. Identify the flavor of the help offered to you. Discern what motivations color that help. Then, choose.

Help comes in five flavors: physical, mental, emotional, material, and spiritual. Here are examples of each:

1. **Physical Help.** Driving on a rain soaked road, you swerve to avoid a moose. Your car skids over the side of an embankment and tumbles into a ravine. Alive, but stunned, you're pinned inside the vehicle. The motorist behind you stops, scrambles down the slope, pulls you out, carries you back up to the road, and shoos away the moose.

2. **Mental Help.** You're a musician, struggling to write a song for an upcoming recording session. The right arrangement eludes you and you abandon the composition. Later in the day, you jam with your band. A guitarist plays a chord sequence and explains why it works. This triggers your thinking about the harmonic structure in your original song. You revise the composition and eventually it goes platinum.

3. **Emotional Help.** As you roll down the hall to the operating room for open-heart surgery, a nurse holds your hand, tells you that

you're stronger than most people half your age, and reminds you that your doctor is world-renowned for this procedure.

4. **Material Help.** After a financial calamity, you have dinner with a friend to discuss your plight. By dessert, you receive a list of potential new customers for your services. While walking home, you discover a check in your coat pocket, inserted by your friend without fanfare, just in case you need some extra funds.

5. **Spiritual Help.** You may wonder about this flavor. I do. Miracles occur, but not predictably. Why are some prayers answered and others not? I just don't know. Closeness to your God may provide you with tremendous solace or inspiration or hope – a unique form of comfort and aid. I leave it to you to reconcile the topic of help with your religious faith.

You may also ask, "What about medical help?" Essentially, healthcare professionals are help providers. They deliver physical, mental, and emotional help, often fortified by extraordinary technology and remarkable pharmaceuticals. Care rendered by internists, surgeons, psychiatrists, physical therapists, and many other talented specialists may greatly boost your recovery from a big loss. I am not a physician and offer no medical advice here. But, I urge you to counsel with doctors and other caregivers, as a normal part of your quest for help, to determine if their treatments can provide the flavor of help that you need.

Help arrives invited and by chance. Help may come in

a single flavor, but more often appears as a mixture. Mental help may accompany emotional help, which may accompany material help. You get the idea because you have plenty of your own examples.

Help rarely arrives in a bolt of lightening. People provide help. Who helps you matters. More importantly, why people offer help to you matters. What motivates them? Why do they want to help you?

Here, we could easily detour into an eyeball deadening discussion about the inherent goodness or badness of humankind. But, people are too complex and history is too replete with devils and saints for me, at least, to make any practical decisions based on the general predictability of human nature. You should avoid this philosophical swamp, too. If you stereotype human intent, you will either accept all help as charitable or reject all help as ulterior. Neither is correct.

Understanding why people offer help to you is important for one practical reason: Not all help is worth taking. If a person proposing help has hurtful intentions, you may be better off rejecting the offer. And, not all help is free. Some help carries an implied debt, an obligation you owe to others for the aid they provide. What if the price is too high?

All help is tinted by the motivation of the person offering it. Help comes in two colors: benevolent and conditional. These colors cannot be mixed. Help is either one or the other. Here's how to judge:

Benevolent help is transparent, pure, genuine assistance. It is a gift with no strings attached. People who provide you with benevolent help do not want to threaten, humble, subordinate, or obligate you. Just the opposite is true. Benevolent help is another person's way of saying, "I respect you." Why else would someone offer you assistance and expect nothing in return?

Benevolent help derives from love or kindness or perhaps just a kindred empathy for your loss. Imagine the death of your affectionate and loyal companion, your sixteen year old cat. Sad and lonely, you share a cup of tea and tears with your neighbor. Later in the day, she returns to your doorstep with one of her kittens for you to cuddle. That's benevolent, emotional help.

Epic loss sometimes accompanies benevolent help – epic because the person suffering the loss is also the person providing the help. Consider the battlefield medic, maimed by a sniper, while bandaging a wounded buddy. Or, consider the educator, bullied by bigots, for tutoring minority students. True heroes risk personal loss to provide benevolent help.

Surprisingly, benevolent help abounds. Many people *do* want to help you. They do. They want to help you because at some point in their lives, *they* needed and benefited by help provided by others.

After each of my major losses, I received extraordinary help from people who also had suffered large defeats. After my Russian fiasco, for example, I was penniless, unemployed, and full of self-doubt. A former client, the head of a major corporation, hired me. Years later, I asked this well-known executive – now a mentor and close friend – why. Here's how he replied: "When I was twenty-four years old, the restaurant that I owned burned down, my brother died, and my wife died leaving me with two infant daughters. I needed all of the help I could get." Then, he looked straight at me with the slightest twinkle in his eyes and added, "Anyway, you were the best candidate for the job." I understood.

Everyone who loses big joins the same club. It's not a very exclusive club because, inevitably, everybody qualifies for admission! Many people who win after losing remain acutely aware of their membership – and never forget how help fueled their recoveries. Sadly, when you lose, you will encounter incorrigible souls who make disingenuous offers to assist you or take bizarre pleasure in your suffering. But, you will also meet many fellow club members who "get" what you are going through and benevolently try to assist.

Asleep after suffering a major loss, you dream about benevolent help. It's risk free, exactly what you need. Awake, seize it without hesitation.

In contrast, conditional help is tinted with a cost or shaded with an obligation. The person offering assistance to you wants something in return. It's not a gift. It's help for a price.

You're already accustomed to paying for help. A bank loan is a good example of conditional help. The bank president may love you, but still expects you to repay the loan plus interest. In fact, if you have ever purchased an insurance policy, you're even willing to pay for help *before* you suffer a loss that *may never occur!* In both cases, the price of help is clear enough for you to select confidently.

But sometimes the price of conditional help is more subtly colored. Consider this situation: You're good at your job and work hard. But, a co-worker gets a promotion that you believe you deserve. Shortly afterwards, your boss suggests that the next promotion can be yours, provided that the two of you "get to know each other a little better." What does that mean?

The price of conditional help ranges from innocuous to onerous. When you think of payment, you naturally think of money. But, beware. The currency for conditional help has a wider spectrum and includes intangibles, such as your self-respect. Try hard to understand the true shade of conditional help by examining: What, precisely, constitutes the payment? How large is the payment?

How long does the payment last? And, what happens if you don't pay?

You and I may view the cost of conditional help differently. What's innocuous to you may appear onerous to me. We don't need to agree. Trust your own color vision to select the right help for you.

Use your independence
to welcome help astutely.

Suppose the conversation in my father's bedroom went this way:

"How are you feeling?" I ask. "You don't look so hot."

"No, I don't feel good," he replies. "I hurt all over. These white pills make me nauseous and these green ones make me groggy. I can't believe this is happening to me. And, I'm sorry to put you through it." He pauses, looks away, and shakes his head. "How are you doing?"

"I'm hanging in there, but it's tough. I'm sad because I know you hurt. And, I'm angry because I can't do a thing to make you feel better. But, I enjoy keeping you company."

I'm silent for a moment. I look at him, trying not to remember what I see. "Are you scared, Dad?"

"Yeah."

"Me too."

What really changes when the façade of lies disappears? Plenty. You let the outside in. All pretending dissolves. The stress of lying evaporates. Your frailties show. But, so do your inner strengths. People come closer. They trust you. They want to help you. Your mind becomes freer, more tranquil, more capable of selecting the right help.

In real life, the right help is not always sufficient. Some losses are impossible to cure. Lies or truth, cancer can't discern. Winning, you understand, is relative. Sometimes, the best you can do is attain small wins within the confines of an inevitable disaster. But, even then, letting the outside in embraces you with the inner peace you crave.

Did this Chapter stimulate you? Share your specific thoughts, questions, and experiences with other readers of **WINNING SMART** AFTER LOSING BIG by logging onto www.robstearns.com. Then, go to the Forum page, select "Chapter Six: Let the Outside In" from the Forum List, and join the discussion.

CHAPTER SEVEN
WHO, NOT WHAT,
YOU ARE

I can see the road perfectly through the hole in the floor of my car. I'm amusing myself by first looking out the windshield, spying something on the onrushing roadway, and then trying to spot the same object through the hole as the car and I zip over it. Somehow, I failed to notice this rust eaten region of the transmission hump before I made the purchase. I confess I was distracted.

Not an aficionado of early Toyota Tercel, I was disadvantaged from the start. The mud orange exterior paint appeared to be original, but several aerosol sprayed swatches on the hood didn't look stock. Neither did the non-matching front seat on the passenger side, which upon later inspection, proved to have Chevy Vega pedigree. The lack of carpeting anywhere in the vehicle seemed Spartan, but not all that suspicious. I did severely test the radio volume control several times and determined that it operated flawlessly. Post-purchase, though not altogether displeased with mandatory sitar, I deduced that on this particular model, the standard equipment list did not include channel selection. The interior smelled faintly of wet cardboard or wet dog, musty but certainly better than, say, Limburger or even Stilton.

Fortunately, the mechanicals made up for any minor cosmetic blemishes. No perforated muffler could account entirely for the confident growl emitted by the car's big block, inline four. The brake squeal indicator worked perfectly every time I decelerated. Steering, especially to the left, was extremely responsive. And although the warranty expired nineteen years ago, the odometer showed just under 88,000 miles.

I bought the car for less than what I used to pay for one month of garage space rent in mid-town Manhattan. In fact, that pretty much summed up my purchase rationale. Several weeks prior, a large bank that had extended me credit while I was flying high invited me to repay in full. The timing seemed right to liquidate all of my remaining assets, including an exquisitely restored Rolls Royce convertible and, for more practical use, a Porsche. You can understand why I bonded with the vintage Tercel immediately.

Absent air conditioning, I appreciate the supplemental breeze provided by the orifice in the floor. I'm driving to meet a friend for a round of golf at his extra-starched, New England country club. The Tercel and I roar past the welcoming fieldstone pillars. I step on the gas, already keenly aware of the vehicle's penchant for uphill momentum. We ascend the gracefully arced entrance lane, magnificently shaded by leafy old oaks, and leave just the faintest flatulence of blue exhaust smoke to drift towards the swimming pool.

Zooming through the circular driveway in front of the traditional Colonial-Federalist-Antebellum clubhouse, I eschew valet parking and head straight for the Members and Visitors lot, a veritable NATO of new automotive hardware. I sidle the Tercel perilously close to the vacant "Reserved - Club Manager" space and turn off the key. Several seconds later, the engine knocks itself out. The Eagle has landed.

When I speak to people about losing, the question that I am most frequently asked is, "What will my children think of me?" A close second is, "What will my spouse think of me?" A slightly distant third is, "What will my friends think of me?" That's why I am eager to talk with you specifically about how your losing affects your interactions with your family and your friends.

Here's the essential message:

You are the same person after your loss as you were before your loss.

People who genuinely loved you before your loss, will continue to love you afterwards. You may not love or even like yourself very much after losing, but I urge you not to impute your feelings about yourself to the hearts of your family and friends. People who genuinely care for you rarely measure you in the same way that you measure yourself. Their love or affection for you has very little to do with your win/loss record.

Your children are a prime example. By losing, you naturally believe that you are letting them down. And as a result, you infer that they are disappointed in you and love you less. No way. Your children love you because you are Mom or Dad, not because you were Vice President of InterOblivion Industries, not because you were rich, not because you were beautiful, not even because you were healthy. Their love for you has no on/off switch, activated when you win or lose. As you flail within the whirlpool of a major loss, I know this sounds too good to be true. Until, of course, you realize that your love for your children is not conditioned on their victories or defeats.

You should talk to your children about your loss. Not with unbridled anger or sadness or fear. But, truthfully and with a level head, the complexity of your message obviously tailored to your children's ages. Children are remarkably perceptive. Unless you are an extraordinary actor, they see through your lie that all is well when, indeed, all is not. They wonder what you're hiding, conjure up the worst, and silently question why you do not trust them with the truth. Uninformed, their logic leaps to blaming themselves for contributing to your loss.

Save your children from the stress of this incorrect conclusion by discussing your loss calmly, but genuinely. Children might as well understand that, in the grown-up world, even the best parents sometimes lose. Just as in the schoolyard, even the best children sometimes lose. The key is that your children sense no panic in your message. Honest but controlled emotion, fine. But, your children see you as a source of security, their first line of defense against the unknown. When you discuss your loss, make sure they feel comforted that you are striving to recover. And, most importantly, tell them explicitly what they absolutely need to hear: No loss can ever diminish your boundless love for them.

Your relationship with your spouse requires just as much nurturing. Your spouse is your equal. Losing does not signal the moment to alter that balance. Your spouse deserves direct communications from you in real time about your loss.

With good intentions and a tad of self-preservation, you are often tempted to insulate your spouse from the distress of your loss. But this pseudo-protectiveness produces exactly the opposite result. Misinformed, your spouse becomes an unwitting roller coaster passenger. The careening ups and downs of any major loss are plenty disconcerting, even when you have your hands firmly on the throttle and the wheel. Imagine how your spouse feels with no control at all and, worse, no understanding of why the ride started and when it will stop.

You can't fool your spouse for very long. Why even try? He or she intimately knows you, inside and out. And, despite your imperfections, he or she still loves you. True, your current loss may test the strength of that love. But, adulthood entitles your spouse to assess that love at any time. And, your spouse deserves to know everything that you know about anything that affects your marriage. Disguising the loss from your spouse is tantamount to admitting that your mutual love is too frail to test. That's trouble, rooted in matters far afield from the specifics of your current loss.

In a marriage bonded by love, crisis coins trust. Tell your spouse everything. Yes, sharing your loss may upset you, your spouse, and your marriage. But, not sharing your loss denigrates your partner and exacerbates a pre-existing weakness in your union. Ask your spouse for help. Always take the risk to obtain nourishment from the people who love you.

Losing starkly identifies your true friends. Expect to be surprised. Expect most of your buds, your pals, your posse, the guys, the girls, the crowd, the gang so full of chatter, high-fives, backslaps, smiles, nods, whispers, and giggles to stampede for the hills moments after you drop the ball. Nothing personal. You just can't do much for them any more.

And though you hurt as you watch their backs recede into the distance, don't holler for their return. They are acquaintances of convenience. When you recover, many will re-emerge to seek your grace, oblivious to how desertion reveals motive. You decide whether they are worth your time again.

But, also expect several loyalists to stick by your side as

you drop defeated. And, take heart that they are not always the people you would predict to hang tough. Cherish these stalwarts for the rest of your life. When they lose, hurry to help them. They are your true friends.

**Your children, your spouse,
and your true friends
love you
for who you are,
not what you are.**

After our round of golf, my friend and I stood on the flagstone patio, overlooking the sacred eighteenth green. We sipped fresh, icy lemonades and exchanged quiet confidences. Later, my friend politely strolled with me to the parking lot. He chuckled when the Tercel initially refused to unlock. He shook my hand with a firm grip as he jocularly said good-bye. And, after that cheery parting, he never, ever called me again.

During their inaugural rides in the Tercel, my grade school sons laughed and excitedly kicked the seats as we bounced over potholes and reverberated through tunnels. My wife mirthfully dissolved while recalling her own first car, a plaid-seated barge allergic to humidity. What we were driving didn't seem to matter. Much to my amazement, they were just happy to be riding with me.

Did this Chapter stimulate you? Share your specific thoughts, questions, and experiences with other readers of **WINNING SMART** AFTER LOSING BIG by logging onto www.robstearns.com. Then, go to the Forum page, select "Chapter Seven: Who, Not What, You Are" from the Forum List, and join the discussion.

CHAPTER EIGHT
HOW TO THINK, WHAT TO DO

Garlic and sizzling butter waft from the kitchen each time the swinging door opens. I'm eating linguini with clam sauce in a ten table, Italian restaurant. It's a local joint alive with throaty laughs, heavy forks clinking against thick white plates, and Sinatra swinging from somewhere in the ceiling. Most of the perspiring waiters and regular diners greet each other by first name. Strangers get a welcome-home, long-lost-brother hug from the Neapolitan owner. Across the white paper tablecloth is a friend. This is a place to talk sports and tell secrets. We're doing both, discussing the lives of my friend and a mutual friend.

We talk first about the athlete. We relive the drudgery of practice, the exhilaration of competition, the pride of playing on an Olympic hockey team. After the anthems and applause, returning home to develop real estate seemed dull, too easy. But, it wasn't that simple. Handsome, well-educated, charming, he floundered. Always so close, he could never quite complete the sale. He smoked dope and drank beer, concocted grand plans, and struggled to make ends meet. Still dazzling on skates, he despised his job, abused his friends, and hated himself. Minor frustrations tormented him. His applause came from acid, his cheers from cocaine. And after each ovation

rushed a depression so unfathomably heavy, so impene-
trably black that one day, he could not stand the thought
of another tomorrow.

Then, we talk about the minister. We relive the arduous
refinement of a tenor voice, the joy of sharing a song on
stage, the satisfaction of performing in the leading role.
But, Hollywood is a long trek from summer stock.
Talented and determined, he could not land a part. HIV
stole his body. Cancer bargained for his soul. Rejection,
fear, and self-doubt turned him to religion. In a hospice,
he ministered to dying men, but never believed his own
words. His comfort came from vodka, his confidence
from cocaine. And after a week-long binge of self-esteem,
he awoke in a puddle of his own vomit and could not
stand the thought of another tomorrow.

Sadly, one of these men pressed the barrel of a gun to
the back of his skull and blew a bullet through his brain.
The other man painfully detoxified, sought therapy, and
now thrives as a media executive. Can you predict who
will win after losing? Are you sure? Then tell me, who is
eating pasta with me – the athlete or the minister?

Eventually, after suffering a major loss, you ask yourself one, haunting question: "Do I have what it takes to
recover?" You look for a sign, some indication that con-
firms your ability to overcome the numbing paralysis of
defeat. But most of the time, the heavens are mum. Expect
no trumpet fanfare. No horizon-shimmering rainbow.
No arcing shooting star. Expect no sign at all to verify the
absolute truth: Yes, you do.

You already have within you, all of the character necessary to win after losing. This character – you might call it
spirit or strength or faith – is deep inside. You were born
with it. You need no book or school to teach it to you,

only the will to find it. I have never encountered anyone without it.

So, stop believing this blather: Losing is good for you because losing builds character. Total nonsense. Losing is never good for you. And, no one in their right mind would choose defeat over victory just to get a whopping dose of character enhancement. I can think of many ways to become a better person other than by getting beaten to the turf. In fact, sometimes losing dissolves character. That's why people cheat.

If you need a mantra, here's a better one: Losing demonstrates character. Less catchy, but more exactly stated:

Winning after losing
demonstrates character
you already have
and *choose to use*.

You are innately equipped with plenty of character. Every day, your strength, resiliency, and resolve triumph over a bombardment of small defeats. You don't ask, "Am I strong enough, resilient enough, resolute enough to recover?" when you experience each minor loss. You know with instinctive certainty that the answer is, "Yes."

Character is not measured in gallons. Defeat doesn't pump more character into you. Your character stays constant, regardless of the size of your loss. Your daily victories prove that you have plenty of character – and that it's potent stuff.

The character that gets you through your normal day is the same character that powers your recovery from a huge defeat. What's unpredictable, after a major loss, is not whether you have enough character or the right character. You do. What's unpredictable is whether you can willfully tap your reserves while confused by great emotional and mental duress.

Every day you recreate order from chaos without even thinking. Entering your darkened bedroom, you automatically reach for the light switch on the wall. Dizzy after a whirling amusement park ride, you instinctively grab for a solid handhold. You confidently recover from these minor confusions because you know, beforehand, the precise location of the light switch or your companion's steadying arm. When you experience disorientation during a small loss, you naturally seek a known or sure solution. Big losses are no different. Stunned and certainly afraid, you seek a familiar and proven way out.

Submariners bet their lives on this reflex. Under hundreds of feet of water and nestled close to nuclear megatonnage, crews repeatedly practice recoveries from simulated, on-board disasters. Ostensibly, these drills permit the submariners to experience and overcome major losses. Over time, their response becomes routine. When a real crisis hits, they reflexively seek a familiar, proven way out.

Even if you are not literally under water, the probability of suffering a major loss during your lifetime is exactly one hundred percent. And figure, with the same certainty, that this loss will confuse and nauseate you. Clearly, you should anticipate and prepare for this sure eventuality. A befuddled "Now what?" is a terrible first response to a big defeat. Instead, your first response should be instinctive, a reassuring gravitation towards safety. To recover from a big loss, you, too, need a familiar escape route.

Winning after losing
begins before you lose.

So is this it? Is this the point in the book where I feed you the magic pabulum? The super-simple, five-step, no-sweat, recipe for triumph? Regrettably, no. I wish it existed, for I surely would share it with you. But, the fact is, winning after losing big is cruelly difficult. Here's why: All of your practice occurs in real time. No simulations exist for major personal catastrophes. True, you can try to anticipate all of the disasters that lie ahead. And sometimes, particularly when you have an inkling of a specific impending defeat, you can rehearse an effective recovery before your moment of doom. But, worrying about your potential losses is a full time job. And even if you could envision and catalog them all, no simple-to-digest slop will guarantee your recovery.

Getting back up after a major loss is not a sure thing. There is no easy fix. You need to work excruciatingly hard. This is not the time to put your trust in smiley faced, rah-rah, feel-good platitudes. This is the moment to face reality starkly and demand – yes demand – that every bit of your mental and physical strength propel you along an arduous path. Everyone who wins after losing big treks this route, perhaps nourished and cheered along the way, but never carried.

In the dark, when you are dizzy, you must find the beginning of this path. That's why, in the prior chapters, I explored the terrain of losing with you. Your familiarity with defeat will enable you, reflexively, to locate this trailhead. In a sense, I provide the compass and a general map. You do the walking.

The path to winning after losing requires that you

think and *do*. Here's how to *think*:

✷ You must consciously want to recover.

This sounds obvious, but the key word is "consciously". If your biochemistry is altered by substance abuse or disease, the physiology of your thinking process simply may not permit you to make rational judgments about your condition or your future. For you to recover from a big loss, some shred of clear thought needs to penetrate whatever mists shroud you.

As we savor dinner in that little Italian restaurant, my friend recalls waking up seven years ago. He remembers jumbled cravings, chills, and most oddly, a piercing desire to end his life. A sliver of rationality sparked an acute sense of danger. He knew that more of the same would kill him. He knew that he did not want to die. He knew that he needed rescue.

✶ You must take a chance and believe that you have the character to recover.

Despite my assertion that you have plenty of character, you still may not fully buy my logic. Fair enough. But, you sacrifice nothing by taking this leap of faith. Rather than critiquing and doubting your internal fiber while under siege, bet on yourself by assuming that you have what it takes to win.

My friend's landlady picked his lock after not seeing him for a week. She found him in bed, barely conscious. She offered help. This time, her offer provoked no thrown glass, no hurled invective. My friend nodded, gratefully. She propped him up, helped him dress, supported him as they descended the stairs. Then, she drove him to the hospital. He remembers wondering if he could survive the nightmares ahead.

✕ You must be willing to recover incrementally.

Big losses often occur unexpectedly and fast. Naturally, you want to recover with equal speed. More than likely, you cannot. Recovering after a major loss almost always requires a series of small wins rather than one or two big ones. And, these small wins are often interrupted by small defeats, as illustrated below in Exhibit 6.

Exhibit 6: Illusory vs. Incremental Recovery

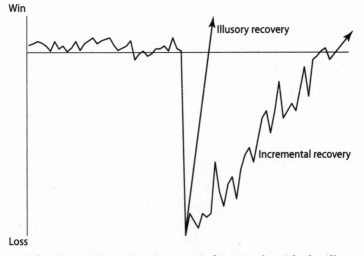

After losing big, it's easy to confuse truth with the illusion of what you hope truth to be. Most opportunities to win big are long shots under the best of circumstances.

After suffering a major defeat, these long shots look enticing because you rosily, rather than coldly, calculate the odds. Beware. Trying to achieve an instant recovery after a major loss puts you in long, long shot territory.

Equally as essential, winning incrementally fortifies your self-respect and your resolve to get back up. If you take pride only when you reach your penultimate goal, you limit yourself to just one instant of victory, one split-second of hard earned gratification. Why treat yourself so harshly? You deserve more. Applaud yourself every time you struggle towards your ultimate recovery, even if you advance just a small step closer. Winning smart is a festival, albeit interrupted, of small wins.

In the hospital, my friend received treatment. His mind cleared. His spirits improved. Discharged, he took heavy doses of prescribed medication. He became depressed, dropped weight, collapsed, re-entered the hospital, and expired in the operating room. The doctors revived him. He participated in a clinical trial of a new pharmaceutical with ninety-nine other patients. All of them, except my friend, died.

✄ You must flexibly define "win."

Winning looks different, depending on your vantage point. When you're wealthy, you may define winning as purchasing a luxurious vacation home. But, if a stock market tumble wipes out your fortune, you may redefine winning as putting groceries on the family table. When you're healthy, you may define winning as learning how to ride a horse. But, as you recover from a stroke, you may redefine winning as regaining the use of your right hand.

After a major loss, you need to refine, pragmatically,

your definition of "win." Is winning recovering every-thing that you lost? Part of what you lost? More than what you lost? Must you win in the same endeavor that dealt you defeat? Or, should your next win occur in a completely new undertaking? *You* decide. But, under-stand that your definition of "win" on the day before you lose may change on the day afterwards.

My friend puts his fork down on his plate mid-twirl, grins modestly, and takes the time to chat with a well-wisher. After the newcomer departs, my friend remarks on how losing big changed his perceptions of other people. He is now more tolerant, more receptive, more for-giving. Few of his current acquaintances know his histo-ry. And, he no longer seeks to recreate past glories in the present. He defines winning in the context of his current health, his current job, his current relationships.

Here's what to *do*:

You must make a plan – simple, flexible, measurable.

Pause, not for long, and breathe. Then, produce an action plan that provides you with a realistic shot at recovery. No need to write a detailed or eloquent script. But, take time to answer some important questions. Feel free to add or delete from these:

- **What is your primary objective?** What are your other objectives?

- **How urgent is your situation?** How much time do you have before your predicament worsens? What will happen if you do noth-ing?

- **What are the "unintended" consequences of your plan?** What are the consequences if your plan fails?

- **What resources do you need to implement your plan?** How can you obtain these resources?

- **Who can you count on to help you?** What will you ask them to do? What if they cannot accomplish what they promise?

- **What large hurdles could disrupt the execution of your plan?** What is the likelihood of encountering each of these hurdles? How do you intend to overcome them?

- **As you implement your plan, how will you measure your progress?** What will you do if your progress falters?

- **What are your personal strengths?** How will you fully use these strengths?

- **What are your personal weaknesses?** How will you prevent these weaknesses from derailing your efforts?

- **Have you ever experienced or observed situations similar to your current predicament?** What worked then that is worth repeating now? What should you now avoid repeating?

- **What is your contingency plan if you cannot execute your primary plan?** What parts of your contingency plan should you execute simultaneously with your primary plan?

Winning after losing is complex and may take a while.

But, the most elegant plan is the one that permits you to achieve your objective in the simplest way. Your plan should be straightforward and brief. You need an outline, not an encyclopedia, to crystallize your thoughts. Measure each element of your plan by its realistic probability of success. Avoid all unnecessary complexity. Clarify. Simplify.

Recovering in the hospital and at home, my friend used the time to plan. He assessed his strengths and weaknesses, thought hard about activities that brought him happiness and success, reflected on events that led him astray. He made lists of people to call, potential occupations to explore, health treatments to investigate. He attached priorities to tasks and assigned tasks to specific dates. And once he separated dreaming from planning, he felt completely comfortable doing both.

You must act.

Curiously, many people have trouble winning simply because they stop after the planning stage. Fear, embarrassment, laziness, and inertia frequently stymie action. But, recovery from a major loss requires your active intervention. Random good luck may help you. But, you sure can't depend on it. And while patience and a cool head are admirable, do not confuse these traits with passivity. You must execute your plan. Only your action will translate your plan from theory to reality. Deeds, not words, fuel your next win.

Medicated and mentally refreshed, my friend went to the gym and built strength and stamina. He launched his search for a job. He contacted acquaintances and asked for help. Several months into the nitty gritty, he received a return call from a woman he had met during the summer more than twenty years ago. They had remained in sporadic touch. Currently the head of a communications company, she offered him a relatively junior position. He accepted without hesitation, worked hard, honed his skills, proved his talent, and now, after several years, continues to ascend the corporate ladder.

———————

Truthfully, you cannot recover from all losses. You may tailspin uncontrollably, numbed by drink or drugs or disease. And, someday you will die, perhaps unknowingly, probably involuntarily. But, after every major loss, as long as you can find the familiar path, you can lift yourself from the depths of despair and regain a portion – perhaps just a small portion – of whatever you seek.

Often, traveling the path becomes a life's work. We sip ice water as we talk, counting our blessings for catastrophes averted, for recoveries achieved. No wine tonight. My friend, the minister, is totally dry.

Did this Chapter stimulate you? Share your specific thoughts, questions, and experiences with other readers of **WINNING SMART** AFTER LOSING BIG by logging onto www.robstearns.com. Then, go to the Forum page, select "Chapter Eight: How to Think, What to Do" from the Forum List, and join the discussion.

CHAPTER NINE
YOU WIN

If you had the power, would you eliminate losing from your life completely? Of course you would. Losing is never one of life's great experiences. You will never get accustomed to losing. You will never enjoy losing. You will never ask for more.

So, how about avoiding loss altogether? Suppose you squint into the future acutely, think dispassionately, and act moderately? What if you shun risk, reject experimentation, and follow paths straight and smooth? Can you insulate yourself from agony by forfeiting pleasure? Can you weave a cocoon invulnerable to life's tempests?

Not a chance.

In the real world, the eventual sure bet is: You lose. You will continue to lose. Your children will lose. And, their children will lose. Losing is a normal part of being alive.

But, so is winning after losing. There is a rhythm to losing, then winning, then losing, then winning, then losing, then losing, then winning, then winning. No particular beat is inevitable. This cadence is unique to each of us. You will win more effectively after losing if you recognize the rhythm and not fear it, confront the rhythm and not flee it, embrace the rhythm and not fight it.

You will win after losing. Summon your strength. Rely on your wisdom. Unleash your imagination. You lose because you are human. You win because you are *you*.

Did this Chapter stimulate you? Share your specific thoughts, questions, and experiences with other readers of **WINNING SMART** AFTER LOSING BIG by logging onto www.robstearns.com. Then, go to the Forum page, select "Chapter Nine: *You* Win" from the Forum List, and join the discussion.

APPENDIXES
WHAT IF?

I wrote this book after thinking hard about my own debacles and reflecting on the inescapable phenomenon of losing. I believe, strongly believe, that my counsel to you is correct. But, it is one man's view and you are entitled to differ.

And, that's the problem with communicating through a book. The path of conversation is one-way. I talk to you. But, I cannot hear your response. I hope that you are cheering, applauding, or just nodding your head in recognition of the truth plainly told. But, I do understand that you may have a question or two. And, it's unfair really, that I am insulated by the book covers while you are eager to start a dialogue.

I suspect that the questions you want to ask relate to your own specific losses. How would I use this book? What would I do if I were in your situation?

Unfortunately, I cannot fully address your questions without knowing more about you and your setbacks. But, in a general way, I can demonstrate how I would use logic from the previous chapters to help think through the five major losses that can knock you flat. In the "What Ifs" that follow, you will find some familiar principles weaved into the text. These highlight moments when your understanding of this book should come alive. The principles really say, "Hey, think about this *now!*"

The problem with general examples is that they miss the nuances and complexities that distinguish your specific losses. Still, the "What Ifs" are plenty valuable if they provoke you to marry the messages of this book to your own, real life recoveries. Winning smart after losing big requires you to reflect and to act. I offer the "What Ifs" to you as a launching pad for both.

APPENDIX A
WHAT IF YOU LOSE A LOVED ONE?

Dark, deep into night, a telephone jangles you awake. You grope for the the receiver, mumble a greeting, then pulse with adrenalin. Dry mouthed, you heave as you are summoned to the hospital. You sit by your husband's bed and listen to the commingling of his breaths with your own. The quiet rhythm, his and yours, in and out, waltzes with your heart. You float until a syncopated silence interrupts your trance. No matter how expected, the end and the beginning always take you by surprise.

The death of a loved one numbs you to the core. The loss is excruciating. Irreparable. Permanent. You're stunned, distraught, angry, and viscerally frightened by your own mortality. But most of all, you're sad, so very sad.

You weep for your loved one's loss of life and the eternal void that now exists in yours. You cry at the stark, immutable divide that isolates your deepest love. And saddest of all, you grieve for opportunities now irrevocably lost to say what you should have said, do what you should have done.

But, perhaps no phone call interrupts your sleep. And, the deathbed furnishes only a bad dream. Then, time remains to preempt those haunting, missed moments. Your second chance exists in the present, before your sorrow begins.

Commune with the dead while they live. Give your spouse the withheld kiss, your child the extra praise, your parent the word of thanks. Forgive all meaningless trans-gressions. End all petty feuds. Express the whole of your love while your loved one can hear and feel and, for your sake, acknowledge. Do this as if you may never have another chance. For indeed, you may not. **Winning after losing begins before you lose.**

Removing your husband's shirts from his shelves, you catch a whiff of his scent and almost believe that he will return home. You bag his clothes, leaving the closet bare. But later that day, you return and discover a pair of his brown shoes standing unlaced sentry in the middle of the closet floor. How did they get there? And as you pick them up and hold them, grateful for the unexpected con-tact, you wonder if you can recover from such suffocat-ing loneliness. **Winning requires no emotional con-stant.**

You ricochet from memory to memory. You stare at the photograph of him, his head tilted just a bit to the right, eyes sparkling, his laugh just emerging as you snapped the shot. You wish you could step into the picture, hug him, hear his happiness. A choking feeling wells up in your throat, but you steady yourself, thankful for the flood of joy that oddly dilutes your sadness. A strange calmness surrounds you. **Understanding and managing your emotions after a major loss is a win.** You place the photograph down on the table, not forever, but for now. Images of him waft through your mind as you begin your day's work. **To turn away from the past and face forward, you must consciously elevate thinking above feeling.** You concentrate, not always successful-ly. **You must be willing to recover incrementally.** You struggle through this day and the next. Grief tugs you backwards. Sometimes you surrender. More often you resist. **You must consciously want to recover.** You focus on your daily routine. You begin to think about your life ahead. **You must make a plan – simple, flexible, measurable.**

Immediately after his death, family and friends bombard you with sympathetic concern. You appreciate their efforts, but wish they would all just leave you alone. And, when they do, you crave their company. **To win after suffering a major loss, you need the help of other people.** You worry that you will burden all who offer help. Will they tire of your tears, your reminiscences, your occasional silences? **Use your independence to welcome help astutely.**

You know, of course, that you cannot resuscitate, recreate, or replace him. He uniquely nourished you, uniquely made you whole. You will never find an exact substitute for the love you shared. **You must flexibly define "win."** You will always miss him. Yet, you discover joy from other people, Nature's beauty, and memories within you.

You are thankful for his presence in your life. He would understand your darkness, but would wish you sun. Perhaps you hear him speak these thoughts as you sip your tea and view the dawn and feel the lightening of your heart. **When you are knocked down, you must force yourself to get back up.**

Did this Appendix stimulate you? Share your specific thoughts, questions, and experiences with other readers of **WINNING SMART** AFTER LOSING BIG by logging onto www.robstearns.com. Then, go to the Forum page, select "Appendixes: What If?" from the Forum List, and join the discussion.

APPENDIX B
WHAT IF YOU LOSE YOUR HEALTH?

Close your eyes and imagine that the last thing you saw is the last thing you will ever see. You are blind. Recall the worst stomachache you ever experienced, multiply it by ten, and imagine it never goes away. You have colon cancer. Run up a dozen flights of stairs until you gasp for air and imagine breathing like that forever. You have asthma. Remember the painful stiff back that once prevented you from standing straight and put that pain and stiffness in every joint of your body, everyday, forever. You have arthritis. Relive the joy of witnessing the birth of your child, then the despair of watching your mother die and repeat that oscillation three times an hour for the rest of your life. You are a manic-depressive. Deprive yourself of sleep until your mind dulls, then pirouette until you are dizzy, and imagine that is the best you will ever feel. You are heavily medicated.

Initially, you ignore the symptoms of your deteriorating health. You are tough. Or, scared. When they recur or worsen, you begrudgingly accommodate your lifestyle. You are resourceful. You do a little reading, perhaps you surf the Internet. You are not surprised when your doctor diagnoses what you already suspect. But you think, "It cannot be because it should not be." You demand more proof and the answer to, "Why me?" **To create a**

win after a loss, you must recognize first that you have lost.

You become human inventory for a medical production cycle. Tests. Treatments. Bills. Co-pays. More tests. To others, your identity morphs from your name to your disease. Inside, you struggle to keep the two distinct. **To create a win after suffering a big loss, you must define precisely what you lost.**

Losing your health is the ultimate loss of control. Your body, the essential chemistry of you, lets you down. You blame other people, fate, and ultimately yourself for your weakness and vulnerability. **To create a win after suffering a big loss, you must respect yourself.** In most cases, though not all, your illness is the result of pure Random Misfortune. **To rebuild your self-respect, you must recognize why you lost.** You did nothing at all to invite this suffering. A microbe multiplied. A gene expressed. And now you are a stranger to yourself, trapped in flawed organs or a discombobulated mind. **Your immediate mission after suffering a loss is to create a win.**

You are outraged, angry, frustrated, sad. **Understanding and managing your emotions after a major loss is a win.** You filter your daily activities and dreams for the future through the tolerances of your disease. You strive to master your illness, then concede to co-exist. **How you *think* about losing and winning is more important than how you *feel* about losing and winning.** Every twinge, every cough, every pill, every detour from your daily routine reminds you of your imperfection. You struggle to stay calm, but occasionally boil over. You wonder if tomorrow will be better than today. Sometimes, you wonder if there will be a tomorrow. **Winning requires no emotional constant.**

You apologize to your children for your lack of energy,

make excuses to your spouse for your dulled desire, avoid activities with your friends to conceal your frailty. You worry that you are a stick-in-the-mud, a burden, an unwanted obligation. You feel isolated in your body, physically near yet light-years distant from those who know you best. You gamely try to spare them, yet covet their comfort. **To win after suffering a major loss, you need the help of other people.** You imagine that you are replaceable. **Your children, your spouse, and your true friends love you for who you are, not what you are.**

Eventually you reach a crossroad, a chance to narrow or widen the gap with your loved ones. They hope for your invitation to come closer, but respectfully await your signal. **You must honestly acknowledge your loss to other people to obtain their help.** You hate admitting that your condition constrains your activities or limits how you think. **You are totally self-reliant only when you can depend on yourself to select help from other people.** But, you understand the value, to you and to the people who love you, of treating your malady together. **You create independence by using it.**

Your health loss may kill you, agonize you, or merely inconvenience you. Recovery may be impossible, improbable, or imperfect. **You must flexibly define "win."** You understand the difference between feeling better and getting better. Despite your fatigue and frustration, you push yourself hard. **You must consciously want to recover.** You reap joys from the everyday. And your very existence nurtures those who love you. **When you are knocked down, you must force yourself to get back up.**

Did this Appendix stimulate you? Share your specific thoughts, questions, and experiences with other readers of **WINNING SMART** AFTER LOSING BIG by logging onto www.robstearns.com. Then, go to the Forum page, select "Appendixes: What If?" from the Forum List, and join the discussion.

"Let's be friends." When you hear these words uttered by your relationship partner, usually spoken softly and reinforced by a tender yet non-suggestive touch, your inner voice instantly responds, "Sure, that's a great idea." Then, you think, "Wait a moment. We've been going out for seven weeks (or "living together for seven months" or "married for seven years"). We're already friends. Whadya mean, 'Let's be friends?'"

A nanosecond later, you get it. "Let's be friends" – the internationally recognized semaphore. Code for: "Let's not see each other any more" and "Let's not sleep together any more" and "Let's not spend any more time with each other because there is something about you that I can't stand and I unilaterally declare our relationship over, done, finished."

Of course, "Let's be friends" is a gentler severance than coming home to find that your partner has tossed all of your worldly goods onto the driveway, hinting "Get out!" Or the reciprocal, opening your front door to find your residence stripped bare, except for your clothes, last night's pizza shards and soda dregs in the refrigerator, a "How Did We Do?" survey card thoughtfully propped by the movers on the bathroom sink next to your solitary toothbrush, and your puzzled dog – all suggesting your partner's permanent exit. And even that pales against the stomach churning discovery of the love-of-your-life flaunting the charade of your relationship by cavorting with a new Mr. or Ms. Right without first having the decency to give you the heave ho.

Whether you are a love-tender teenager or love-grizzled adult, losing a relationship takes your breath away. The feeling in the pit of your gut is always the same. Another human being, someone with whom you entrusted and shared mental and physical intimacies, someone who enthralled you, dazzled you, made you laugh, made you cry, made you remember, made you forget, someone whose tomorrows seemed ordained to entwine with yours . . . that someone awoke one morning and extrapolated a future that no longer included you. And no matter how you received the message, you feel naked, duped, abandoned, angry, and absolutely stunned by the rejection. **How you *think* about losing and winning is more important that you how *feel* about losing and winning.**

Getting dumped is so hard to swallow because it is so totally, inescapably, acutely a rebuff of you. Not your performance at work. Not your lack of some particular charm or talent. But a spurning of you the person, the complete and entire you. Somehow, your ex-partner tallied up your good points and your bad points, assessed the difference, and determined your eternal incompatibility. Regrettably, your ex-partner may be right. Or not. Either way, the blow-up of the relationship leaves you alone to ponder "What did I do wrong?" **To create a win after suffering a big loss, you must respect yourself.**

Quite naturally, you revisit the life of your relationship and search for clues. You remember past occurrences, past conversations, benign at the time but in retrospect, clear foreshadows. Perhaps you ignored your partner's requests or signals. Perhaps your partner could not or chose not to meet your expectations. Perhaps the indescribable chemistry that brought the two of you together could not sustain the bond. You may never unearth a wholly satisfactory explanation for your partner's decision. But, your search may reveal at least the source of the relationship's unraveling. **To rebuild your self-respect, you must recognize why you lost.**

Still, the void haunts you. A distant silhouette, a familiar chuckle, a melody, a rainstorm snaps you from the present to the past. Your knees turn to jelly as you contemplate a phone call, a letter, an apology, an admission, a reaffirmation, a plea. But, you realize that these attempts will yield the same silence as all of your previous tries. **To turn away from the past and face forward, your must consciously elevate thinking above feeling.** You stop staring at old pictures, stop re-reading old notes. You make yourself supper on a Saturday night and almost enjoy the quiet. **Understanding and managing your emotions after a major loss is a win.** As you wash the dishes, you wonder if you will ever find another person to accept the best and worst of you.

Relatives and friends introduce you to a gaggle of new people. Chance encounters abound. But you resist, worried that your anger and disappointment will mask the love you hope to share. **Winning requires no emotional constant.** You procrastinate, fearful that any new relationship ultimately will dissolve. **You must consciously want to recover.** You claim you're "just not ready" to search, to play the game, to recommit. **You must take a chance and believe that you have the character to recover.**

A close friend telephones you with rave reviews about "someone you must meet." You're deservedly skeptical. Last week's saint refused to use cutlery. Two weeks before, there was the "kayak," "my yak" mix up. Kid stuff compared with that searing pain in your broken big toe, last month's prize for a gymnastic tango with "someone who can really dance." **You must be willing to recover incrementally.** Still, you're curious about the person and also about yourself. You already know that the unflawed partner and the perfect you live only in fairy tales. **You must flexibly define "win."**

Your friend convinces you to take a chance for only an hour on neutral turf. **To win after a suffering a major loss, you need the help of other people.** On the appointed day, you consider feigning the flu and backing out. But, you compel yourself to attend. You enter the room and jostle through the convivial mob. You spot your friend talking with some familiar faces and a stranger in the corner. You approach, engage in introductions, catch the twinkle in the stranger's eyes, and hear a new voice say gently, "Hi." **When you are knocked down, you must force yourself to get back up.**

Did this Appendix stimulate you? Share your specific thoughts, questions, and experiences with other readers of **WINNING SMART** AFTER LOSING BIG by logging onto www.robstearns.com. Then, go to the Forum page, select "Appendixes: What If?" from the Forum List, and join the discussion.

APPENDIX D
WHAT IF YOU LOSE YOUR JOB?

Getting fired is particularly insulting. What could be more demeaning than being told, probably by a dolt of the first magnitude, that you're inadequate, you're dispensable, and even worse, you're disposable. Sure, the messenger delivered the bad news civilly. But, what you really experienced is the three-hundred-pound ump, eyes piercing a black iron mask, sweating under a hulking chest protector, springing out of his crouch, twirling emphatically over one leg, pumping his thumb high in the air, and bellowing, "Yerrrr Oouutt!" All that's missing are the "booos" – and you may hear them later.

You absorb this insult on several levels. Intellectually, you question the obvious misjudgment of your competence and value to the enterprise. Emotionally, you resent the failure of your employer to return the favor of your invested loyalty. And, from deeper within, you feel intensely sad about the personal rebuff. The termination notice, minus the legalese, essentially says, "You smell."

After the immediate outrage washes over you, incredulity, then disorientation, then maybe a bit of panic hits you hard. This is certainly not in the imaginary script that directs your life along perpetually happy trails. How old are you? Twenty-five? Just about ready to buy that first house. Thirty-five? Trying to save for the kids' college tuitions. Forty-Five? Bolstering the care for your elderly parents. Fifty-Five? Tough to convince employers that you still burn intensely. Sixty-Five? Too expensive and too difficult to train. The timing is never right for this outrageous ad lib.

Let's back up. **Winning after losing begins before you lose.** Suppose you haven't lost your job yet. Suppose you're worrying about losing your job. Unless you're looting the till, you rarely get booted without some prior inkling. Whatever the cause – you just can't add, your department is over staffed, you're clumsy with explosives, your boss hates you – you should have some clue when your neck is on the block. **To prevent a loss, you must recognize first that you are losing.** What are you doing to preserve your job? Can you work harder, longer, smarter, better, differently, or for someone else? Or, is it too late? **To create a win after a loss, you must recognize first that you have lost.** If so, then what are you doing, before the pink slip arrives, to get another job? **You must make a plan – simple, flexible, measurable.** You prepare your resume, identify potential employers, survey the job market in your industry and in acceptable geographies. **Your immediate mission after suffering a loss is to create a win.**

Canned. Sacked. Terminated. Downsized. Gasping for air, you head home. You replay various moments on the job that, in retrospect, marked the turning points. Blood pressure rising, you concoct remedies – perfect, but for a time machine. You revel momentarily in the thought of your foot on the throat of your nemesis. An hour after the fateful farewell conversation, you mouth the words you really wanted to say at the time. **To turn away from the past and face forward, you must consciously elevate thinking above feeling.** You calm yourself and begin to think about your obligations and your future.

Taking a harpoon to the groin was painful enough. But, now you must admit your collapse to your spouse. **Your children, your spouse, and your true friends love you for who you are, not what you are.** Over dinner, you talk honestly, admit your fears, and respond attentively to questions. You and your spouse, together, assess the financial implications of your job loss. Together, decide how to reduce spending immediately. Together, prepare for the long haul.

Asleep as a child, did you dream about installing carpet? On balmy spring afternoons, did you daydream about becoming a bond trader? Catching your reflection in the mirror, did you ever preen and say, "You. You can be a clerk?" I doubt it. My bet is that the job you just lost fed you, but did not nourish you. **To create a win after suffering a big loss, you must define precisely what you lost.** For certain, providing for yourself and your family is tough and requires sacrifice. But, as you hunt for employment, can you better combine your economic needs with the fulfillment of your dreams? **You must flexibly define "win."**

For a while, depression saps your energy. Crescendos of "What did I do wrong?" interrupt mealtimes, lovemaking, and all attempts to find solace. Perhaps you did nothing. Maybe you contributed mightily to your own ejection. **To rebuild your self-respect, you must recognize why you lost.** You examine your behavior, your performance, and honestly accept your fair share of responsibility for the loss.

You identify friends who can help you find your next job and confide in a select few. **You must honestly acknowledge your loss to other people to obtain their help.** You seek their advice. You do your homework. **You must act.** You ask for specific assistance. "Jim, I would appreciate it if you would help me," isn't specific enough. It's a blanket plea, not an actionable request. Try "Jim, would you introduce me to your friend who owns the ice cream plant?" Provide ammo. "I sold a million cases of vanilla last year and I have great relationships with several large, local buyers." **To win after suffering a major loss, you need the help of other people.**

Though you try to do everything right, you meet with disappointments. You stumble in an interview. People promise to call you back, and forget. The position you coveted gets filled, and not by you. You persist. For those who depend on you. But really, for yourself. You make the extra calls, knock on more doors, tap inner reserves of grit until you hear, "You're hired." **When you are knocked down, you must force yourself to get back up.**

Did this Appendix stimulate you? Share your specific thoughts, questions, and experiences with other readers of **WINNING SMART** AFTER LOSING BIG by logging onto www.robstearns.com. Then, go to the Forum page, select "Appendixes: What If?" from the Forum List, and join the discussion.

APPENDIX E
WHAT IF YOU LOSE YOUR MONEY?

Feel free to ignore anyone who tells you that losing all of your money isn't so bad. This well-intentioned pap usually comes wrapped in words that mean: "It could be worse." Of course it could be worse. Your child could die. You could go blind. Loss of life and health obviously overtrump loss of material goods. But, losing your fortune often generates stresses that endanger your physical and mental health and jeopardize your family's welfare. Unfortunately, "It could be worse" almost always proves prophetic. A major financial calamity often foreshadows an onset of "worse."

Really, how much money you lose does not describe the magnitude of this loss. What makes this loss so gigantic and so stunning is that you have lost it all. You have substantively nothing left. Zero is the great leveler. You have no wiggle room, no grubstake, no down payment for the present or the future. You cannot buy your way out of petty nuisances or even begin to protect against major disasters. Every expenditure – rent, medicine, pet food, a pair of socks, a pack of gum – requires you to ration. **To create a win after suffering a big loss, you must define precisely what you lost.**

You initially consider the carnage of your investment portfolio as just a "paper loss," a momentary detour outside yesterday's financial heaven. You easily concoct scenarios where boom times return. You muffle the bad news and amplify the faintest, optimistic glimmer. **To recognize when you have lost, you must consider your measurement standards so sacred that you do not ignore them or change them conveniently in times of crisis.** But the truth is, your savings are gone. And so is the future that you worked so hard to secure for yourself and your dependents. You painfully downsize. You offload luxuries and forego conveniences to afford the basics. You rely on tomorrow's wages to pay for today. **To create a win after a loss, you must recognize first that you have lost.**

You never imagined that you would be penniless. But, your net worth is only part of your torture. Your self worth is bankrupt, too. You look in the mirror and wonder how you could be so stupid, so careless, so lazy to permit your savings to evaporate. **To create a win after suffering a big loss, you must respect yourself.** What should you have done differently? Which assumptions led you astray? **To rebuild your self-respect, you must recognize why you lost.** You initially blame "the market" or your advisors. And maybe you are right. But, you are also smart enough to question the inevitability of perpetual good news. And deep down you know that betting and investing are not the same. **To rebuild your self-respect after a self-inflicted Execution Failure, you must accept undeniable and sole responsibility for the loss.**

You feel terrible. Overwhelmed. Small. **How you *think* about losing and winning is more important than how you *feel* about losing and winning.** You replay the financial disaster in slow motion, over and over. Yes, in retrospect, you should have preserved your assets. But you did not. **To turn away from the past and face forward, you must consciously elevate**

thinking above feeling. Recovery in the future, not undoing the past, is at stake. **Your immediate mission after suffering a loss is to create a win.** Starting again at square one seems impossibly difficult. You wonder if you have the strength, the stamina, the resolve that enabled you to succeed in the past. **Winning after losing demonstrates character that you already have and *choose to use*.** You review and revise your budget and honestly discern your genuine needs from your discretionary wants. You mull "How much is enough?" and respond differently than when you were king of the hill. You discover that your answer largely depends on the height of your hill and whether you are climbing or tumbling. **You must flexibly define "win."** You wish you could get even immediately and crave the chips necessary to make a big bet. At the same time, you are gun-shy, reluctant to rely on the intelligence and prudence that powered your previous victories. You size your expectations realistically and establish an achievable pace. **You must be willing to recover incrementally.**

You have plenty of time to recover incrementally because while you are struggling, numerous former acquaintances conveniently forget your telephone number or fail to include you in social gatherings. To some, you are your balance sheet. And possibly, you once measured yourself that way, too. You are different after losing your fortune because you realize that you are not different at all. **You are the same person after your loss that you were before your loss.**

In unfamiliar financial territory, your barometrics seem brontosaurial. You rely on your experience, but also seek fresher perspectives. **To win after suffering a major loss, you need the help of other people.** You solicit counsel from several advisors and carefully segregate hype from insight. **Use your independence to wel-**

come help astutely. You build your savings again, dollar by dollar. You focus on details and demonstrate discipline enough to prevent small financial losses from snowballing. **To prevent a loss, you must recognize first that you are losing.** You begin to build a cushion, patiently, purposefully, and probably slowly. You focus on "How?" rather than "How much?" **When you are knocked down, you must force yourself to get back up.**

Did this Appendix stimulate you? Share your specific thoughts, questions, and experiences with other readers of **WINNING SMART** AFTER LOSING BIG by logging onto www.robstearns.com. Then, go to the Forum page, select "Appendixes: What If?" from the Forum List, and join the discussion.

APPENDIX F
THE PRINCIPLES OF WINNING SMART

CHAPTER ONE

Only people lose and win.

**The forging of trust
occurs in the crucible of loss.**

CHAPTER THREE

**When you are knocked down,
you must force yourself
to get back up.**

**Your immediate mission
after suffering a loss
is to create a win.**

CHAPTER FOUR

**To prevent a loss,
you must recognize first
that you are losing.**

**To create a win after a loss,
you must recognize first
that you have lost.**

To recognize when you have lost,
you must consider
your measurement standards
so sacred
that you do not ignore them
or change them conveniently
in times of crisis.

To create a win
after suffering a big loss,
you must define precisely
what you lost.

To create a win
after suffering a big loss,
you must respect yourself.

To rebuild your self-respect,
you must recognize
why you lost.

To rebuild your self-respect
after a self-inflicted Execution Failure,
you must accept undeniable
and sole responsibility
for the loss.

CHAPTER FIVE

How you *think* about losing and winning
is more important than
how you *feel* about losing and winning.

Understanding and managing
your emotions
after a major loss
is a win.

To turn away from the past
and face forward,
you must consciously elevate thinking
above feeling.

Winning requires no emotional constant.

CHAPTER SIX

To win after suffering a major loss,
you need the help of other people.

To win after suffering a major loss,
you need the help of other people.

You must honestly acknowledge your loss
to other people
to obtain their help.

You are totally self-reliant
only when you can depend on yourself
to select help from other people.

You create independence by using it.

Use your independence
to welcome help astutely.

CHAPTER SEVEN

You are the same person after your loss
as you were before your loss.

Your children, your spouse,
and your true friends
love you
for who you are,
not what you are.

CHAPTER EIGHT

Winning after losing
demonstrates character
you already have
and *choose to use.*

Winning after losing
begins before you lose.

You must consciously want to recover.

You must take a chance and believe
that you have the character to recover.

You must be willing to recover
incrementally.

You must flexibly define "win."

You must make a plan –
simple, flexible, measurable.

You must act.

ACKNOWLEDGEMENTS

Acknowledgment pages are risky. Smarmy accolades anesthetize even the most loyal readers. And, the prospect of forgetting to name someone who deserves recognition makes me sweat. Still, I need to give it a go. How else can I thank the people who love me for who, not what, I am?

At the top of the list is my wife, Katie. An exquisite bouquet of brains, beauty, humor, and intuition, she challenges, motivates, inspires, and understands me. A true partner. Always.

I salute and hug my sons, Aaron and David. They are my buddies in times glorious and goofy. Remarkably accomplished, refreshingly youthful, and distressingly strong, they simply make me want to do better.

I am privileged to enjoy loyal and caring friends who nurture me intellectually and nourish me emotionally. I am extraordinarily indebted to Bill Kristol for thirty years of genuine friendship, Jim Schrager for eclectic wisdom, candor, and trust, David Kronfeld for the honesty and unspoken affection that only a brother can provide, Nick Sakellariadis for always rallying to my call, Tom Luby for unknowingly infusing me with tolerance, and Jim Longley for reminding me, by his example, to join persistence with principle.

I am grateful to John Teets for always keeping his

word, Rick Scott for gracefully standing strong, Mal Jozoff for relentlessly demanding perfection, John Walker for incenting me with breakfasts, Steve Sohn for prescribing proper protective equipment, Geoff Dunbar for repeatedly getting back up, Alan Shalette for insightful critique, John and Ann Syverson for neighborly compassion, Fritz Allis and Hale Sturges for kindling my curiosity, and Herb Kaufman for championing my teaching at Arizona State University.

I applaud Don Schmidt of D.W. Schmidt Co. for artistic creativity and savvy communications counsel, Peter Collier, Steve Wiley, Roger Rapoport, Carol Staswick, and their colleagues at Encounter Books for intelligence and flexibility, and Craig Shirley, Bob Keyser, Kevin McVicker, and their colleagues at Shirley & Banister Public Affairs for effectively spreading the word.

I bow deeply to my stepfather, Sol, caring, tolerant, and the most generous man I know. And finally, to my Mom, who, with unwavering love, spine, and resiliency, has enriched this manuscript and five decades of my prior work. To her, I confess that I never wear a hat.

**HERE'S YOUR OPPORTUNITY
TO GIVE TERRIFIC GIFTS
TO YOUR FRIENDS AND COLLEAGUES!**

ORDER ADDITIONAL COPIES OF

>REVITALIZING PEOPLE, REVIVING ENTERPRISES<

❑ YES! Send me _____ copies of WINNING SMART AFTER LOSING BIG for $16.95 each.

❑ YES! Send me information about Rob Stearns Live Events for my company, association, or enterprise.

Please include $4.95 to cover shipping and handling costs for one book, plus $2.95 for each additional book.

Your payment by check or credit card must accompany your order. Please allow three weeks for delivery.

My check for $_____ is enclosed, or

Please charge my ❑ Visa ❑ MasterCard ❑ American Express

Name_____

Organization_____

Address_____

City, State, Zip_____

Telephone _____ E-mail_____

Credit Card Number_____

Expiration Date _____ Signature_____

Return this form with your credit card information or check payable to:

Encounter Books
665 Third Street
Suite 330
San Francisco, CA 94107-1951

Or call toll-free: **1-800-786-3839**

Or visit: **www.robstearns.com**